Beginner's
ROMANIAN

Beginner's ROMANIAN

Dana Gall
of Eurolingua

HIPPOCRENE BOOKS
New York

Copyright© 1994 by Eurolingua.
Second printing 1999.
All rights reserved.

For information, address:
HIPPOCRENE BOOKS, INC.
171 Madison Avenue
New York, NY 10016

ISBN 0-7818-0208-3

Printed in the United States of America.

TABLE OF CONTENTS

Introduction.. 7
Geography... 9
History.. 12
Arts... 17
Practical Advice for Everyday Life................... 22
Language Characteristics............................. 31
Language Lessons..................................... 33
Lesson One: Meeting People/Introduction.............. 35
Lesson Two: Customs.................................. 40
Lesson Three: Local Transportation................... 46
Lesson Four: Hotel................................... 52
Lesson Five: Going for a Walk/Asking for Directions... 58
Lesson Six: At the Restaurant........................ 63
Lesson Seven: Shopping............................... 71
Lesson Eight: Being a Guest.......................... 77
Lesson Nine: Being Sick.............................. 85
Lesson Ten: At the Business Party.................... 90
Key to the Exercises................................. 94
Vocabulary... 96
Romanian-English Expressions......................... 99
English-Romanian Expressions.........................103

ACKNOWLEDGMENTS

Gratitude and thanks are due, for the inspired suggestions and invaluable help I received, in selecting, putting together and editing the materials presented in this book. Many thanks in this respect to:

> Prof. Mircea Fotino
> Prof. Ileana Vasiliu
> Prof. Ecaterina Mariotti
> Mrs. Giti Samar-Fleischer
> Mr. Chip Baker
> Prof. Mary Jones
> Dr. Sergiu Levin

For her perpetual encouragement and energizing initiatives, special thanks are due to Prof. Katalin Boros, of Eurolingua.

With profound gratitude and appreciation, I also wish to mention the scrupulous advise and unconditional support I received from my dear husband, Ludwig Gall, throughout this venture.

INTRODUCTION

The rich culture and languages of Eastern Europe are unique, intricate and subtle, steeped in tradition by hundreds of years of history. But, since the Eastern European countries were closed societies for over 40 years under communist rule, little is known about them.

After the fall of the Iron Curtain a flurry of activity is being spurred throughout Eastern Europe by the desire to establish democratic institutions and free market economies. Firms from the West are exploring business opportunities and expansion into these virtually untapped markets.

A fresh and beautiful land together with the rich and exciting cultural heritage of its peoples has opened up for tourism to explore.

As a result, EUROLINGUA was started in September 1990 to meet the growing demand for Eastern European language and cross-cultural instruction. EUROLINGUA primarily serves tourists and business people who deal in international trade.

The passionate traveler would like to understand and enjoy the people and the customs of the country he will visit. For a successful international transaction the businessman has to know the appropriate behavior in various business situations. And finally, basic information about geography, history and politics of the country to be visited, together with some language knowledge will make anyone feel at home anywhere.

These considerations have brought about this book, in the hope that it will become your friend and guide during your trip.

Knowledge of customs, manners and some basics of language will help you discover more exciting things and make more friends than you ever dreamed.

The book has two parts. The first part gives you information about the country (geography, history, economy, culture, customs, manners) and the second part consists of language lessons.

The language lessons are designed for the traveler and the non-specialist amateur. You will learn useful phrases and words for special situations and basic grammar hints. The lessons will not cover all grammar problems, nor will they give a rich vocabulary for sophisticated conversation. Instead they will teach you enough to feel comfortable in a variety of situations, which you will find described here.

With this small, compact book you will have in your pocket a collection of bits of information, sufficient to carry out a satisfying interaction with the people of the country you visit, in their own language. It is the result of many hours of work, research and travel done by enthusiastic teachers and travelers, who wish you good luck in your study and a wonderful trip.

GEOGRAPHY

Centered around the 45th parallel of the northern hemisphere and described either as a country of the Balkans, or as a southeastern European country, Romania offers a lot of geographical contrasts. The Carpathian Mountains, covered with dense forests, enclose the Transylvanian Plateau in a wide arc, a distinctive feature, evident at first glance on any map of Romania. On the outside of this arc the Moldavian Plateau stretches to the East and the Wallachian Plain to the South.

The country covers an area of 91,669 square miles. It is comprised in almost equal proportions of plains, hills, plateaus and mountains. Bordering countries are: Moldavia and the Ukraine, two former republics of the now defunct Soviet Union, to the East and North, Hungary to the North-West, Serbia of former Yugoslavia to the South-West and Bulgaria to the South. Romania also has 150 miles of coastline on the Black Sea to the South-East.

The Carpathians, divided as Eastern, Southern and Western Carpathians, average 4,000 feet in height. Their composition offers a rich geological diversity of sedimentary, metamorphic and volcanic rocks. The highest peaks are Moldoveanu and Negoiu (more than 8,300 feet) in the Făgăraş Mountains, of the Southern Carpathians. The mountains are crossed by many rivers: the Olt, the Mureş, the Prahova, the Bicaz, which create beautiful valleys and canyons, such as Turnu Roşu in the Olt Valley and spectacular gorges like the Bicaz Gorge, in the Eastern Carpathians. There are also marvelous caves, the most famous being "Peştera Urşilor". The mountains hold granite and basalt quarries, as well as lead, bauxite, iron ore, copper ore, gold and uranium mines.

Enclosed by the massive walls of the Carpathians, there are depressions, which played an important role in Romanian history. Romanians named them "countries" (the Oaş Country, the Moţi Country, the Olt Country, the Maramureş Country) even though they have never had any political, social or administrative status.

The Subcarpathians form the transition between the Carpathians and the plains. The high hills offer good conditions for orchards, vineyards and hay-making. The soil is rich in coal, salt and oil.

Some of the Romanian plateaus, such as the Transylvanian Plateau, are in the center of the Carpathian arc, others, such as the Getic Plateau, the Moldavian Plateau, the Dobrudja Plateau are on the outside. They are generally covered with beech and oak forests, and vineyards on the gentler slopes. It is on these plateaus, where the famous Cotnari, Odobești, Târnave and Murfatlar vineyards are located.

The Romanian or Wallachian Plain is surrounded by the Carpathians to the West and North, by the Danube River to the South and by the Dobrudja Plateau and the Prut River to the East. It is the "bread-basket" of the country, formed mostly of layers of loess and alluvial soil. On the eastern part of this plain there are some sand dunes, salt lakes and the Bărăgan steppe, some of which was converted into arable land. The Western or Banat Plain in the West is smaller than the Wallachian Plain.

Covering an area of 1,500 square miles the Danube Delta in the East of the country is a unique ecosystem in Europe. It is an extraordinary natural reservation consisting of marshes, sandbanks and floating reed islands, crossed by hundreds of water channels.

Almost all major rivers of Romania flow into the Danube which is the largest river of the country and one of the largest in Europe. It forms the natural border to Serbia, Bulgaria and the Ukraine. It is an important water route for domestic and international ships. A powerful hydroelectric plant was built in 1972 at the Iron Gates straits, where the Danube dug a narrow canyon across the Carpathians, to make its way toward the Black Sea.

Other major rivers are the Olt, the Someș, the Mureș, the Jiu, the Prut and the Siret, some of them being used for local transportation or logging. Most of the hydroelectric potential of the rivers is being utilized. Mineral springs with therapeutic properties have been long in use at Băile Herculane, Băile Felix, Tușnad, Vatra-Dornei, Olănești, Călimanești etc. Many health resorts were built in these areas.

Romania's considerable diversity of fauna and flora derives from the complexity of the relief. One can distinguish the following three vegetation zones: alpine, forests and steppe.

The alpine zone begins at about 5,500 feet and consists of mountain pines, small bushes and shrubs scattered on mountain meadows. The fauna is represented here by the bearded vulture and the chamois.

Romania's forests cover more than 25% of the land. The coniferous forest is intermingled with birches and maples at lower altitude. The Transylvanian Plateau is covered with oak and beech trees. Large oak forests can also be found in Dobrudja, in the

Western Plain, across the northern part of the Wallachian Plain and in the southern Subcarpathians. Large numbers of deer, wolves, bears, lynxes, squirrels, hawks, and owls roam these forests.

The steppe, although mostly cleared for agriculture, can still be found East of Bucharest and in the southern Dobrudja. It is the land of hares and bustards.

The Danube Delta has a special vegetation of reeds and sedges and thousands of birds come here every year.

Romania's climate is temperate-continental, with some local variations produced by the diversity of relief. The hottest months of the year are July and August, with the average temperature of 85°F and the coldest month is January with 25°F. The Carpathians affect the humidity and the winds causing weather modifications. The Mediterranean influence in Romania's south- west and in southern Dobrudja results in mild winters and hot and dry summers.

Administratively Romania is divided into 42 counties (ju deţe). Bucharest, the capital, is the most important political, economical and cultural center of the country. It is situated on the Dâmboviţa River in the south-eastern part of the Wallachian Plain, and is surrounded by many natural lakes and forests. Other major cities are: Cluj, Timişoara, Jassy (Iaşi), Constanţa, Braşov, Sibiu, Arad, Oradea. There are several port cities such as Sulina, Galaţi, Giurgiu, and Orşova on the Danube, and Constanţa on the Black Sea.

The population of Romania is approximately 23 million. Romanian-speaking people represent about 86% of the population. As ethnic minorities, Hungarians and Germans live mainly in Banat and Transylvania, Serbians in Banat, and Jews throughout Romania. The Gypsies form one of the largest ethnic groups. Some of them live a nomadic life, others are settled near large cities like Bucharest and Constanţa. A limited number of Russians, Bulgarians and Turks live in Dobrudja, Ukrainians in Maramureş and northern Moldavia.

HISTORY

The continuity of human settlements in the territory of Romania goes back as far as the Paleolithic period. The diversity of its geographical conditions, its rich fauna and flora played a favorable role in assuring this continuity.

Before the period of Roman domination, various tribes populated present day Romania. The most important and famous ones were the Scythians and the Sarmatians, living in the south-east area, and the Geto-Dacians occupying the northern banks of the Danube and Transylvania. Herodotus mentioned the Geto-Dacians in his account of the expedition of Darius, the King of the Persians, against the Scythians. The Dacians succeeded in organizing a powerful state extending from Transylvania toward the Black Sea and the Danube river.

Their last king, Decebal, strongly resisted the invading Roman legions, but was defeated in 106 AD, when the Emperor Trajan turned Dacia into a Roman Province. The Dacians in the northern part of Transylvania, who were free from Roman dominance, were a permanent menace to the north-eastern Roman Empire.

Following the occupation, 165 years of intense Romanization of Dacia determined the Latinic character of the Romanian language. Christianity also entered Dacia during this time and consequently the basic religious vocabulary is of Latin origin.

The Romanian people are the descendants, through the millennia, of this mixed population of Roman colonists and Dacians.

For the next 1,000 years the Latinic character of the language survived the onslaught of the barbaric migrating people and has been preserved to this day. During all this time, Romanians lived continuously in the territories of Moldavia, Transylvania, the Northern side of the Danube, and Dobrudja on the shores of the Black Sea, farming and raising livestock. Although there was no centralized government during this period, the Romanian people remained true to the Latin origins of their customs, religion, and social laws, while maintaining a strong sense of unity throughout this tumultuous period of their history.

By the end of the 11-th century, the Hungarian kings succeeded in conquering Transylvania by defeating the Romanian "Voivod" Gelu, Glad, and Menumorut living in the northern and western part of Transylvania. "Voivod," a title of Slavic origin, was given initially to military commanders and afterwards to governors of provinces. In the 14-th century Basarab founded the first Romanian state "Wallachia," bordered in the North and West by the Carpathians, to the South by the Danube and to the East by the Black Sea.

His son conquered other territories populated by Romanians north of the Danube Delta, at that time controlled by the Tartars. This region became known as "Bessarabia," after Basarab.

East of the Carpathians another Romanian state "Moldavia" was founded during the same period. The Moldavian Prince Bogdan "Vodă" established its borders at the Dnister to the East and the Milcov to the South, including Bessarabia. However, the Romanian region between the Prut and Dnister remained known as Bessarabia.

Throughout history the Romanians living in Moldavia, Wallachia, and Transylvania considered themselves brothers, spoke the same Romanian language, had the same religion, culture, and customs and always fought to unite in a common state.

A Romanian writer, Eusebiu Camilar, referred to Romania as "the gate of storms." This name is well justified as the following will illustrate. First, Romania was like a buffer squarely in the way of barbarian invasions from Asia, especially the Tartars. The Romanian Princes shouldered this burden keeping the invaders out of their own country, and at the same time protecting Western Europe and its culture. Second, Romania was for Europe the key to all exchange with the East. Third, with neighbors such as the Turks, the Austro-Hungarians and the Russians all of whom were powerful empires at that time, the Romanians had to defend not only their borders, but also their national entity, religion, and culture against being absorbed. Thus, until the unification in 1918, Romanian history was a continuous struggle for national unity and independence for all Romanians. When the expansion of the Turkish Empire and the roaming of the Tartars became a menace to Eastern and Central Europe, they were halted by Romanian princes such as Mircea the Old, Vlad the Impaler, Matei Basarab, Ștefan the Great (described by Pope Sixtus IV as an "Athlete of Christ"), Petru Rareș, Ioan the Terrible, who served as a buffer between these invaders and Western Europe through more than 400 tumultuous years.

The first one to accomplish the centuries old dream of Romanian national unity was Mihai the Brave, who succeeded in uniting

Wallachia, Moldavia and Transylvania in 1599. This state survived for less than one year, but it was burned into the national memory of all Romanians and they never again ceased to fight for unification. Though separated by political borders the Romanians kept their sense of unity, which is reflected in their customs and folk art.

In the quest to extend their spheres of influence, each of the three empires surrounding Romania attempted to conquer, or succeeded in conquering some region of the country. For long periods of time from the 16-th to the 19th century, the Turks were kept at bay through payment of tribute, which sapped the country's wealth.

In 1775 Austria annexed Bucovina, the northern part of Moldavia, and in 1812, Russia took Bessarabia. It was the policy of the occupying forces, to destroy the national spirit of their victims and to assimilate them. In spite of this, language, religion, culture, and customs of the Romanians survived.

In the 19-th century the great ideas and ideals of the 1848 French Revolution inspired the Romanian intellectual elite, which started to work toward unification. Literature and journalism reflected strong nationalistic feelings and the longing for national unity.

In 1859, the first two to unite were Moldavia and Wallachia and the new country was named Romania. In 1866 King Carol the First of Romania was crowned and a new era of economic and democratic development, and stabilization began.

In 1877 Romania gained its independence from the Turks and in 1918, at the end of WWI the most treasured dream of all Romanians was accomplished. Transylvania, ancient Romanian territory was finally united with Romania.

Also in 1918, Bessarabia declared itself independent of Russia and united with Romania. The same year, Bucovina also came back to Romania.

However, during the WWII turmoil and due to machinations of the superpowers, Romania lost Transylvania to Hungary, and Bessarabia to The Soviet Union. It is to the credit of the Romanians that during WWII the Jewish population was well treated and there were few deportations by comparison with the areas administered by the Germans.

Through the peace agreements at the end of WWII, Transylvania was reincorporated into Romania, but Bessarabia and northern Bucovina remained part of the Soviet Union, as the Soviet Republic of Moldavia, suffering a fate similar to the Baltic States and other Soviet Republics.

From this time on, Romania was firmly within the sphere of influence of the Soviet Union, inside the area upon which the Iron Curtain came down. During the years that followed, the communists took hold of and consolidated power and, in 1948, they forced the abdication of king Mihai of Romania, marking the beginning of the darkest and most shameful era of Romanian history.

The communist transformation of Romania's political, economic, and social life was accomplished by the mid 1950s. During this time Romania was a satellite of Moscow.

An important dichotomy characterized Romanian politics under Ceauşescu. On the one hand, its foreign policy evolved quite differently from the ones practiced by the other communist states in the region. The tangible rewards of this phenomenon included memberships in important international organizations, Most Favored Nation trading status in the United States, and high level visits to Romania by Western leaders. On the other hand, Ceauşescu established an extremely centralized administration and a total dictatorship at home. He assigned top party and government positions to members of his family, who were leading vulgar, ostentatious lifestyles, while the vast majority of the population lived in utter poverty. The pauperization process was so intense, that Romania became known as Europe's Ethiopia, as opposed to the monarchy period, when its capital was referred to as Little Paris.

By the late 1980's Bucharest's blatant disregard for basic human rights and the gradual unmasking of Ceausescu's unmitigated dictatorship led western powers to withhold concessions granted earlier.

Romania was the last of the six East European Warsaw Pact states to be shaken by revolutionary changes in late 1989. The collapse of Ceauşescu's regime, however, was far more precipitous and violent than the failure of communism elsewhere. The revolution swept away President Ceauşescu. He and his wife, Elena, were executed following a hastily conducted trial by a military court.

The violent revolution of 1989 proved that the desire for democracy and freedom of the Romanian people was still alive after 45 years of dictatorship.

However, the regime which has emerged, retaining many key figures of the Ceauşescu regime, doesn't honor these aspirations. It has denounced and abolished communism, but its methods of government and treatment of political opposition are similar to those of the dictatorship it replaced. Attributes it has earned for itself, like: neo-communist and "new mask, old faces", are very meaningfully indeed. Reports of human rights violations are numerous, and members of the opposition parties are often harassed and abused.

Despite the repression and misinformation, the political parties which existed in the period between the two WWs, the National Liberal Party, the National Peasant Party, and the Social Democratic Party have been reestablished. Other political organizations formed in the aftermath of the 1989 revolution, today in reluctantly tolerated opposition, are: The Civic Alliance and the New Democratic Convention. Hopes are set high, that eventually this opposition will gain the strength to prevent the abuses of political power, which became the rule under the communists still practiced by their heirs, and to bring about an era of true, enlightened democracy in Romania.

ARTS

The history of Romanian culture may be defined through the perspective of the at times slow, at times tumultuous interaction between tradition and innovation. This interaction, while open to outside influences, generated specific lifestyles and ways of thinking, and determined the perception of the Romanian phenomena abroad.

Having imperial Russia, the Austro-Hungarian Empire, and the Turkish Empire as dangerous neighbors, Romania was a Latin island lost in an ocean of Islamic, Greek and Slavic influences. Under these circumstances, the only way for Romania to exist as a political and social entity, with characteristic cultural values, was to consciously cultivate the past that had granted her national identity.

Because of uninterrupted difficulties stemming from the numerous barbaric invasions coming from the East, Romanians, throughout their history, had to adopt a defensive position. This was a way to preserve their national existence, but it also delayed the process of developing a well-defined literature. A fairly rich folk culture grew instead, representing the self-consciousness of the Romanian people and becoming the source and inspiration for the Romanian literature of the 19-th and 20-th centuries.

For the Romanian shepherd and farmer the nature and the land were an existential element that provided food or offered an escape in case of danger. The Romanian soul will always find its strength in nature. This dependence was expressed in beautiful and unique folk songs, the Ballads. Ballads are the purest expressions of the Romanian collective consciousness, as well as the perfect symbiosis that existed over the centuries between man and nature. They reflected the ancient wisdom of the people. The jewel of the Romanian ballads is "Miorița" (the Ewe Lamb), found in over 900 versions all over Romania thus reflecting the strong unity of Romanian folk culture. The ballad describes the hypothetical murder of a shepherd, in which death is presented as a wedding, and "the after-death ceremony stands for both a way of integration into the cosmos and a strong original solution to the incomprehensible brutality of a tragic destiny."(1)

Because of the tumultuous Romanian history marked by the centuries long invasions of the barbarian populations from the East, and by the long Ottoman rule, the beginnings of a literary language can be traced only as far back as the 17-th century.

Despite the many ups and downs and the political separation between the Romanian provinces the national culture exhibits a harmonious evolution as a consequence of the unity of language and religion.

Over a period of almost two hundred years (16-th to 18-th centuries) the Moldavian chroniclers Grigore Ureche, Miron Costin and Ion Neculce enhanced the idea of the Romanians' Latin origin and thus raised the national consciousness. "The essential synthesis achieved by the Moldavian chroniclers was the factual demonstration of the existence of a "Romanian time", of an uninterrupted history, of a national specific spirituality opened towards the universal."(2)

Through Dimitrie Cantemir, the Prince of Moldavia and an erudite scholar, the Romanian humanism reached its highest peak in the 18-th century and was recognized by many western humanist circles.

Transylvania was not an exception to this awakening of national consciousness. Scholars like Samuil Micu, Gheorghe Şincai, and Petru Maior used culture as a political tool to fight for the liberation of Transylvania so that the great historian Nicolae Iorga considers them "Champions of the national ideal."

Later on, the Romanian romantic writers, composed epic poems, which gave new dimensions to the relationship between the national and the universal. The longing for national unity continued to prevail in the writings of Costache Negruzzi, Dimitrie Bolintineanu, Vasile Alecsandri and Grigore Alexandrescu, who praised the memory of those Romanian Princes, who fought for national independence.

The Romantic exaltation was moderated by the classical atmosphere of the literary society "Junimea" (the Youth), and through its mentor Titu Maiorescu. He tried to clean the literature from the "forms without content" in order to achieve more depth and meaning. His essay "Word inebriations" is a masterpiece of the genre.

One of the members of Junimea was Ion Creangă, an original popular narrator, who wrote fairy tales and "Recollections from childhood." His works are marked by a practical utilitarian perspective inherited from his peasant roots, by his ironic morality, and by his use of popular proverbs, collected from age long folklore. Creangă is the most relevant exponent of the Romanian popular genius through his capability to laugh even during the saddest moments.

Ion Luca Caragiale, playwright, sociologist, and moralist was one of the best interpreters of the mentality of his time. His comedies, "sketches," articles, and short stories reflected his ironical, rebellious, and analytic spirit and gave a modern dimension to Romanian literature.

The supreme genius of the Romanian culture, Mihai Eminescu, synthesized the wisdom and the national consciousness of the Romanian people, its love and worship of nature, the eternal meditation about the mysteries of the universe, and the longing for a lost love. Modern Romanian literary language has its main source in the works of this poet. The greatest of his philosophical poems is "Luceafărul" (the Evening Star) a parable and moral meditation.

Nature and peasant life were themes developed by Ion Slavici, Liviu Rebreanu, Mihail Sadoveanu and, after 1944, by Marin Preda.

Considered by the literary critic Constantin Ciopraga as a "poet of the drama of knowledge," Lucian Blaga is one of the greatest Romanian poets and philosophers.

The communist regime suffocated the artistic talents that were attempting to develop poems other than those imposed by the Party line. Poets like Marin Sorescu, and Ana Blandiana, tried to elude censorship by revealing the truth and criticizing the regime. As a consequence, they were denied publishing rights, but the artistic value of their poems nevertheless places them among the greatest contemporary Romanian poets.

Hidden among the rolling hills of the beautiful Romanian landscape are wonders of old church architecture: little churches and monasteries with marvelous mural paintings of Byzantine influence. The most famous ones are Voroneț and Putna in Moldavia, Curtea de Argeş, Tismana, and Hurezu in Wallachia, and the little wooden churches typical for the region of Maramureş in northern Transylvania. On the exterior walls of Voroneț, murals, unique through the freshness and the beauty of their colors, have weathered the onslaught of the elements for more than four hundred years, perplexing today's experts with their original splendor. The peasant icons adorning these churches display in their styles the rich influence of Romanian folk art. European religious art receives an essential contribution through the quality and imagination, but also through the realism of the Moldavian religious art.

Except for some small regional differences, the Romanian folk art is homogeneous. Beautiful rugs, carved wooden objects and pottery will decorate the Romanian houses. A tradition to carve ornaments into the wooden portals of the house persists in the whole country and primarily in Maramureş (northern Transylvania). They are truly artistic creations. Maramureş is a region rich in folk art. At Săpânţa, the vision of death as a part of life itself inspired the peasant artists to carve on the wooden crosses joyful scenes from the life of the deceased, accompanied by funny rhymes. The "Happy Cemetery" from Săpânţa is now considered a masterpiece of the folk art and is visited by many tourists.

The first documentary evidence of Romanian folk costumes goes back to the 11-th century. Some parts of the folk costume such as the woolen trousers, black high pointed fur cap and the leather moccasins keep their Dacian origin.

The beautiful and artistic hand embroideries, the geometric and floral motives and the predominance of white, black and red are the common features of folk costumes.

Some of these treasures of the folk art can be seen at the "Village Museum" and at the "Museum of the Folk Art" in Bucharest as well as in any village of the country.

The beginnings of Romanian sculpture and painting can be traced back to decorative or rite objects in the churches and monasteries of the feudal period. The 19-th century marked the burgeoning of classical painting. Artists like Constantin Rosenthal and Gheorghe Tăttărescu painted subjects relating to the 1848 revolution. Theodor Aman is considered the first modern Romanian painter. The most famous painters of this century were Nicolae Grigorescu, and Ion Andreescu who painted, scenes from the traditional Romanian life, historic scenes, and landscapes.

Stefan Luchian was the first to bring modern European trends to Romanian painting. Gheorghe Petraşcu, Theodor Pallady, Alexandru Ciucurencu gave new and modern dimensions to their paintings.

At the beginning of the 20-th century, sculpture was represented by artists like Dimitrie Paciurea, Ion Jalea, and particularly Constantin Brâncuşi. He was the most famous Romanian sculptor and his original inspiration won him recognition and appreciation throughout the world. Brâncuşi's themes are inspired by the Romanian folklore and are stylized in abstract form.

The communist period was to be a dark one for all the arts. In order to be published, or to have their works exhibited, artists were compelled to treat political and social themes in a way, that destroyed spontaneity and let their work become a tool for propaganda and Ceauşescu's personality cult. Severe censorship curtailed any inspiration of the slightest inconvenience to the regime.

Principal objects of the early Romanian architecture were churches and fortresses. In the 17-th century the "Brâncoveanu style" was developed during the reign of prince Constantin Brâncoveanu, characterized by large porches supported by stone pillars, doors and window frames decorated with floral motives and rich carved ornamentations. The "Mogoşoaia Palace" near Bucharest was built in the Brâncoveanu style.

The architecture of churches and other public buildings displays some Russian influence in Moldavia and German influence in Transylvania.

In the 18-th and 19-th centuries the architecture was strongly influenced by the western style visible in many buildings in Bucharest and other cities. Ion Mincu tried to halt this trend by developing a new style in the tradition of the Romanian folk architecture.

The Romanian folk music had a strong impact on contemporary music. Anton Pann, a writer and folklorist, was the first to collect and popularize the Romanian folk music. By the end of the 19-th century Ciprian Porumbescu composed vigorous patriotic songs with strong Romanian character.

Composer, conductor, and violinist George Enescu was the first Romanian musician of international fame. Many of his works, such as the "Romanian Rhapsodies" and the "Village Suite" develop themes from Romanian folk melodies. Another musician of international fame was Dinu Lipatti, an outstanding classical pianist.

Romanian music was enriched during this century by the works of composers like Sabin Drăgoi, Mihail Jora, Alfred Alexandrescu, Mihail Andricu, Dimitrie Cuclin, and Pascal Bentoiu.

Conductors such as Ionel Perlea, and nowadays Sergiu Celibidache, are well recognized names on the international music scenes.

At the dawn of a new millennium, the Romanian culture is trying to get out of one of the darkest periods of its history, seeking to regain its place on the universal scene.

(1) Ciopraga, Constantin "The personality of Romanian literature"
                          Junimea Publishing House, 1981, p58
(2) Ciopraga, Constantin "The personality of Romanian literature"
                          Junimea Publishing House, 1981, p25

PRACTICAL ADVICE FOR EVERYDAY LIFE

1. LOCATION

The towns in Romania are densely populated, with crowded streets and most people living in high rise apartment buildings.
   The layout of major streets is not in a systematic north-south/east-west square pattern as in the U.S.A. Streets always have names, never numbers. Directions are given according to well known tall buildings and other landmarks instead of using the points of the compass. Distances will be specified in meters or kilometers (one meter equals 3.3 feet and one kilometer equals almost 2/3 miles). Expect misunderstandings when asking for directions. It is always good to have a map.

2. GROUND TRANSPORTATION

a. Public Transportation

The most common way to reach your destination is by using public transportation. In major cities one can choose between bus, trolley and tram, while small cities offer only bus routes. The tickets must be purchased in advance at ticket counters, newspaper stands or tobacco shops. You may have to wait in line, so it might be a good idea to buy a larger quantity, since the tickets don't have an expiration date. The passenger must validate the ticket upon boarding, by using one of the hole-punching devices mounted throughout the vehicle. Employees of the public transportation company will perform occasional spot checks. Anyone caught traveling without a valid ticket will be fined.
   Buses, trams, and trolleys are often crowded and/or late (random schedule). They usually don't operate between about midnight and 4 am. Pushing and shoving during the boarding process is the rule, but, as long as it is within certain limits, nobody gets upset about it. Entrance and exit doors are seldom respected, especially during rush hour.

A subway is available in Bucharest only. There are several major routes, so it is likely one will have to switch on a longer trip. A map of the metro lines should help with better orientation. The metro is fast and reliable but you cannot enjoy any sightseeing. It operates 24 hours a day.

b. Taxi

The most comfortable way to move around is by taxi, which is recommended for tourists who are not familiar with the areas. There is a state owned company with cheaper (metered) rates, but with only a small fleet, which cannot meet the demand. Private cabs fill the gap, but they don't use meters, so the fares should be negotiated in advance. Competition will sometimes drive down the price.

c. Trains

For travel between cities the most common means of transportation is the train. Trains are operated by the C.F.R. (the Romanian Railroad). For long distance travel (more than 100 miles), there are international trains and express trains, called "rapid" and "accelerat." The "personal" train is very slow, because it stops at every little village and is used mostly for shorter distance commuting. One has a choice between first and second class, and some night express trains have sleeping cars. Basic comforts are not comparable to American standards, even in first class, due to lack of maintenance: no heat, no A/C, sometimes no light. Trains often run behind schedule, sometimes by hours. Crowded trains are the rule and it is advisable to buy the ticket with seat reservation in advance (2-3 days up to 2-3 weeks). This has to be done at the counter and is a cash transaction. A phone call to the travel agent won't do. It is good to bring your own food and drink on the trip, because restaurant car service is not reliable.

d. Buses

If your destination doesn't have a train station, or if the train schedule doesn't suit you, bus service, which covers almost every village, will take you there. The bus terminals are called "autogara." For long distances passengers are accepted only within the available seating. Only on shorter routes standing is allowed while riding the bus. Therefore try to reserve seats in advance.

e. Car

If you decide to drive, consider first the poor road conditions. Highways are narrow, badly maintained, soiled by agricultural traffic and usually have only one lane in each direction (there is only one four lane highway: between Pitești and Bucharest). Markings have probably not been renewed for years and working street lights are the exception at night. You will likely encounter horse drawn vehicles and people walking or riding loaded bicycles in shaky balancing acts.

Gas stations are scarce, open on a limited schedule and often one has to wait in a long line. Gas is sold by the liter (1 US gallon equals 3.78 liters). There is no self serve and the attendant expects a tip for just putting gas in your car. Service stations are also scarce and many Romanian drivers are used to do almost all minor (and sometimes major) repairs on their own.

Be very careful in traffic. The going driving style is aggressive and unpredictable. At any unmarked intersection yield to vehicles coming from the right. Within city limits the maximum speed is 60 Km/h as a general rule and lower where indicated. On rural highways the speed limit may be up to 100 Km/h, depending on the type and HP of your car.

When renting a car, an international driver's license might be required. Check the car out thoroughly (make sure the spare tire is there!) before departing and have any irregularities recorded in the contract. Ask about the A.C.R. (the Romanian Automobile Club) location and available services (technical assistance, medical assistance) and ask for the "Tourist and Motor Car Map," where you will find every gas station marked. You may be able to obtain gas stamps, which might assure you priority service at gas stations.

f. Airport

Airports are usually crowded. Pushing and shoving at the ticket and check in counters are more often the rule, than waiting in line. Take care of all documents you receive when entering the country, you'll need them when you'll exit. So far the only carrier on Romanian national routes is "TAROM"- the Romanian Airlines. They charge foreigners in hard currency, but are still inexpensive.

3. CURRENCY

Leu (leu -sg. and lei- pl.) is the Romanian currency. It has 100 bani as subdivisions. Currently there are bills of 10, 25, 50, 100, 500 lei and coins of 25 bani, 1, 3, 5, 10 lei. Foreign currency and traveler checks can be changed at the National Bank of Romania and some hotels, and exchanges can be refunded, but sometimes there are problems with this, and all the receipts should be kept. Presently there are no ATM machines. It is advisable to carry cash in small change ($ 1, 5, 10, 20 and coins), Don't rely on credit cards or personal checks. Major hotels might accept them but not restaurants. Usually, if buying something with traveler checks, you will receive the change in local currency.

4. SHOPPING

Although trends toward privatisation started after the 1989 revolution, most of the stores are still owned by the government. Small specialized stores (clothing, food, souvenirs) and small restaurants or bars opened in the private sector. Store opening hours are quite different from those in U.S.A. There is no 24 hours store in Romania. Usual opening times are as follows:

Mon-Fri. - 6:30am - 9:00pm. - grocery stores (Alimentara) and they might be closed for lunch between 12 - 2pm.
- 9am.- 9pm. - some big department stores (Magazin Universal)
- 9am. - 6pm. - other regular stores with one hour lunch break at noon
Sat. - 6:30am - 6 pm. - grocery stores
Sun. - 6:30 - 9 am. - some grocery stores
- most other stores will be closed
(Stores are also closed on official holidays.)

There is no sales tax added to the prices displayed and one has to bring one's own bag to carry the purchased items. Sometimes, especially in state owned stores, if the change is less than 1 leu, the clerk often rounds it to his favor.

There are also shops with payment in hard currency, some of them in hotels, but they are more expensive.

When purchasing electrical appliances one must know that in Romania the standard voltage is 220 Volts. An adapter is required for an electrical device designed for 110 V to be operational.

There are specialized food shops for bread, meat and dairy products. To get fresh vegetables and fruit one has to go to an open-air vegetable market where only seasonal produce is available. Everything is sold in metric units:

1 kg.= 2.2 lbs., 1 meter = 3.3 feet, 1 liter =.26 gallon.

5. RESTAURANTS

There are no restaurant chains or drive-through's in Romania. Also, do not expect to find restaurants offering foreign ethnic cuisine. Only few restaurants have separate smoking and non-smoking areas and usually you will seat yourself. The average Romanian cannot afford to eat out very often, it is rather a luxury.

With few exceptions, there are seldom more than a couple of choices on the menu, and sometimes you won't receive a menu. You won't receive water unless you ask for it, and generally there is no ice-water.

Romanian restaurants serve mostly meat based foods. There are no salad bars. The salad is served together with the main dish and there are no multiple choices of dressings.

The coffee is very strong (Espresso or Turkish) and not always pure. Alcohol is served to anyone over the age of 18. Try some of the famous wines of Murfatlar (Pinot Noir or Pinot Gris), Cotnari or Muscat Otonel and "țuica" a strong plum brandy.

The tip is not included in the bill so when you pay, usually to the waiter, include the tip too (10 % - 20 %).

It is a good idea to verify in advance the business hours of restaurants.

There are self-service restaurants: "bufet expres" or "lacto-vegetarian" but of questionable quality. The "cofetărie" serves cakes, soft drinks, coffee and ice-cream. The soft drink might be soda with orange aroma and might have several names: "suc, citro, oranjadă, limonadă, răcoritoare," sometimes pepsi-cola.

When starting to eat it is customary to wish "poftă bună" (good appetite). It is proper to hold your knife in the right hand and the fork in your left hand throughout the meal. Cut one bite of food at a time, do not chop it up in advance and then switch your fork to your right hand in order to eat.

6. RECREATION

While on your trip, you can continue with your exercise routine. All the cities in Romania have many beautiful parks, where you can jog and some major cities have tennis courts available. Riding the bicycle might be dangerous due to heavy traffic but you can enjoy it on small streets or in rural areas.

The most popular sport in the country is soccer. There are many professional clubs and several championship leagues. Children and/or adults playing soccer in parks, playgrounds or sometimes on quiet streets are a common sight.

Other popular sports in Romania include volleyball, basketball, handball, water polo, tennis, track and field, gymnastics etc.

The beautiful mountains offer great conditions for climbing in summer (Retezat, Bucegi, Parâng) or for skiing in winter (Poiana Braşov, Sinaia, Semenic, Parâng, Păltiniş). In summer the beautiful "Delta Dunării" (Danube Delta) offers excellent conditions for fishing, boating and wild life observation. The Black Sea coast just south of the Danube Delta is lined with a string of lovely sea side resorts and wide sand beaches.

7. INTRODUCTION / FAREWELLS

Greetings and introductions are more formal and guided by rules than they are in America. It is customary to introduce a younger person to an older person, a gentleman to a lady, a subordinate to a superior. Shake hands while telling your last and first names. Address your new acquaintances by their last names (using Mr., Mrs. or Ms.).

Sometimes, as a sign of respect, a man will kiss a woman's right hand. Most likely older persons will do this, but younger men might do it as well. Children often greet older persons with "sărut mâna" and it is customary as an old-fashioned formal greeting for a gentleman to greet a lady the same way: "sărut mâna" (its literal translation means "I kiss your hand") and at the same time he may reach for the lady's hand and gently kiss it.

8. VISITING

When you are invited for lunch or dinner it is polite to bring small gifts: flowers or a bottle of wine and sweets for children. Also try to be on time or no more than 15 minutes late; if later you should call.

Meals are bigger than they are in America so be prepared to eat a lot. The glass if empty will be refilled without asking permission. To avoid a situation where you have to refuse an insistent host you may want to take small sips.

9. COMMUNICATION

The privacy of phone conversations and mail still cannot be counted upon and people are still uneasy about freely expressing their thoughts. Many things are not just a phone call away in this country and many households are not yet equipped with a telephone. Public phones operate by coins and operators are not available 24 hours.

10. PUBLIC SERVICES

There is not one emergency phone number, but separate emergency numbers for police, ambulance, fire. There are no toll-free numbers, no poison line, no support groups. Also there are no drive-through services at banks or restaurants.

11. HOLIDAYS

The following is a listing of the more important holidays observed in Romania. Schools, offices and shops might be closed on some of these days.

January 1 is a holiday. This follows the year's biggest party night.

January 24. On January, 24, 1859, Moldavia and Wallachia were united and the country was named Romania. It was the first step toward the unification of all Romanians.

March 1 is the day when people will give "mărțișoare" to the beloved ones. These are little pieces of crafts representing love symbols and the arrival of spring.

March 8 celebrates the women in the world. Women receive flowers and small gifts.

Easter is also celebrated. Children build grass nests and Easter Bunny will leave gifts there for them: decorated eggs and candies. People eat bacon with cheese, lamb and knock decorated eggs.

May 1 is May Day. Its significance has grown smaller since the collapse of the Ceauşescu regime.

May 9 marks the day in 1877 when Romania regained her independence from the Turks, through the heroic struggle of her army.

December 1 is the national day. In December, 1, 1918 the Romanians gathered at Alba Iulia, in Transylvania, succeeded in accomplishing the most treasured dream of the nation, the unification of Transylvania with Romania.

December 22. On this day the 1989 revolution is celebrated. After more than 40 years of communism, the Romanians overthrew Ceauşescu's dictatorial regime.

December 25 is the Christmas holiday. Trees are decorated, but only on December 24. Santa Claus will come that night bringing gifts for children. Many people go to midnight mass on December 24. That evening children or friends visit each other, sing carols and receive small gifts.

12. EXPRESSIONS OF TIME

Zilele săptămânii (the days of the week)

luni	Monday
marţi	Tuesday
miercuri	Wednesday
joi	Thursday
vineri	Friday
sâmbătă	Saturday
duminică	Sunday

Lunile (the months)

ianuarie	January	iulie	July
februarie	February	august	August
martie	March	septembrie	September
aprilie	April	octombrie	October
mai	May	noiembrie	November
iunie	June	decembrie	December

In Romania, the official way of expressing time is the military format (000-2400)

Example.
Cât e ceasul?   What time is it?
E ora 14.   It is 2 pm.
E ora 21.   It is 9 pm.

Note:
For two o'clock the feminine form of the numeral cardinal is used: e ora **două**./ it is two o'clock.

Minutes can be expressed in two ways:

1. The hour is followed by the word **"și"** and the number of minutes from 1-60.

Examples:
unu și zece (1h 10 min)
șase și douăzeci (6h 20min)
unu și treizeci și cinci (de minute) (1h 35min)
nouă și cincizeci și patru (9h 54min)

2. The number expressing the hour is followed by the word **"și"** and the number of minutes, as above. Optionally, for the minutes in the second half of the hour, the number expressing the next hour is followed by the word **"fără"** and the number of minutes to be added to complete the hour.

Examples:
două și cinci (2h 5min)
trei fără unsprezece minute (eleven minutes to three)
unu fără nouă minute (nine minutes to one)

For 15 minutes often **"un sfert"** is used, for 30 minutes: **"jumătate"** and for 00 min: **"fix"**

Examples:
unu și un sfert - a quarter past one
nouă fără un sfert - a quarter to nine
trei jumătate - half past three
șapte fix - seven o'clock

LANGUAGE CHARACTERISTICS

The Romanian language is a Romance language and developed from the Latin spoken by the intermingled populations of Roman colonists and conquered Dacians in the Roman province of Dacia. In the center of Slavic speaking people, the Romanian language is the only Romance language spoken in Eastern Europe. It developed differently from the other Romance languages French, Spanish, Italian, and Portuguese, but also kept many of the features of its original Latin source. Most of the vocabulary and grammatical structure are Latin, but Slavic, Turkish and Greek influences are also present. The Slavic influence left its mark between the 6-th and 11-th centuries, during the period of barbaric invasions, with words used in agriculture, for animals and social ranks. When the Orthodox religion entered Romania and the Byzantine culture influenced early Romanian literature and rite, new words of Greek origin entered the vocabulary. The long period of control exercised by the Turks would mark the vocabulary too.

During the 19-th century the affinity toward cultures of Latin origin, especially French, determined the adoption in the Romanian vocabulary of many French words, mostly technical terms and expressions of modern social life.

In the present days, because of its Romance character, the Romanian language is closer to the other Romance languages in the West and thus more open to the Western culture.

The Romanian Alphabet

A	a	as in	c**u**p	M	m**a**s in **m**oon
Â	â			N	**n** as in **n**o
Ă	ă	as in	**a**n	O	**o** as in d**o**g
B	b	as in	**b**ig	P	**p**as in **p**ot
C	c	as in	**c**ar	Q	q
D	d	as in	**d**og	R	**r**as in **r**ock
E	e	as in	**e**lse	S	**s**as in **s**and
F	f	as in	**f**oot	Ş	**ş**as in **sh**are
G	g	as in	**g**arden	T	**t**as in **t**en
H	h	as in	**h**ome	Ţ	**ţ**as in bi**ts**
I	i	as in	**i**nk	U	**u**as in c**oo**k
Î	î			V	**v**as in **v**ictory
J	j	as in	rou**g**e	W	wdublu v
K	k	as in	**k**eep	X	**x**ks
L	l	as in	**l**amp	Y	yigrek
				Z	**z**as in **z**ebra

Note:
 1. The letters Â,â,Î,î represent the same sound and it cannot be compared with the sound of any standard English vowel. It is pronounced as a combination between "ee" in meet and "oo" in loop and is articulated with spread lips and the center of the tongue is arched toward the roof of the mouth.

Î, î are used
- at the beginning or at the end of the word
întrebare, înger, întuneric, amărî, coborî

- when the verb is in gerund
văzînd, intrînd, aterizînd

- when a prefix is added to a word starting with î
neînsemnat, preaînălțat, neîntrebat

Â, â are used everywhere else when the letter is in the middle of the word
gât, mâna, mâine, întârziere, român

All these orthographic rules were approved in 1932 by the Romanian Academy. Later, after the Communists took over in Romania they adopted an orthographic reform in 1953, which retained the use of "â" only in words referring to Romania and its derivates and in some proper names. This generalization of the use of "î" was inspired by the reform of the Russian orthography, imposed by the bolshevik linguists at that time. The orthographic reform in Romania aimed to undermine the Latinic character of the Romanian language and to emphasize a parallelism between the Russian and the Romanian phonetic, as perceived by the communists. Consequently, all the books printed between 1953 - 1991, used the letter "î". After the 1989 revolution the Romanian Academy proposed to reinstate the orthographic rules established by the 1932 reform.

2. There are letters that are pronounced differently when they are grouped together.

ce	as in	**cha**mpion
ci	as in	**chi**p
che	as in	**ke**ttle
chi	as in	**ki**ng
ge	as in	**ge**ntle
gi	as in	**gi**nger
ghe	as in	**ga**ve
ghi	as in	**gi**ve

Exercise:
Read aloud the following words:
cine, cicoare, cerneala, cenușa, chemare, chenar, chipiu, chin, gen, lacrimogen, margine, magiun, ghereta, magheran, ghioc

LANGUAGE LESSONS

LECŢIA UNU

A FACE CUNOŞTINŢĂ

În avion

Avionul tocmai a trecut graniţa română. Două cupluri stau pe acelaşi rând.

Radu: Scuzaţi-mă, doamnă, v-au căzut ochelarii. Poftiţi, vă rog.

Ana: Mulţumesc frumos. Sunteţi foarte amabil. Ştiţi la ce ora aterizăm?

Radu: Da. La ora unu şi jumătate. Daţi-mi voie să mă prezint: mă numesc Radu Popescu şi Maria e soţia mea. Ne întoarcem dintr-o excursie în America şi suntem din Bucureşti.

Mihai: Eu sunt Mihai Ionescu şi aceasta e soţia mea Ana. Şi noi suntem români, dar am plecat din România acum cincisprezece ani. Este pentru prima oară că venim înapoi.

Radu: Mai aveţi rude aici?

Mihai: Nu, am venit pentru afaceri, dar vrem să facem şi nişte excursii prin ţară.

Ana: Pot să vă întreb ce lucraţi?

Radu: Desigur. Maria e profesoară şi eu sunt doctor. Dar dumneavoastră?

Mihai: Ana lucrează la o bancă şi eu cu fiul meu ne ocupăm cu comerţul de calculatoare. Dumneavoastră aveţi copii?

Maria: Da. Avem un fiu şi o fiică. Merg amândoi la şcoală. Acum bunica are grijă de ei. Precis că ne aşteaptă la aeroport.

Ana: Priviţi! Aterizăm.

LESSON ONE

MEETING PEOPLE / INTRODUCTION

On the Airplane

The airplane just crossed the Romanian border. Two couples are sitting in the same row.

Radu: Excuse me, Madam, you have dropped your glasses. Here you are.

Ana: Thank you very much. You're very kind. Do you know what time we'll be landing?

Radu: Yes. At 1:30. Let me introduce myself. My name is Radu Popescu and this is Maria, my wife. We were in the United States on a trip and we are from Bucharest.

Mihai: I am Mihai Ionescu and this is my wife Ana. We are Romanians too, but we left Romania fifteen years ago. It is the first time that we are coming back.

Radu: Do you still have relatives here?

Mihai: No, we are on a business trip, but we'd like to see some more of the country too.

Ana: May I ask you what you do for a living?

Radu: Of course! Maria is a teacher and I'm a doctor. How about you?

Mihai: Ana works in a bank and I sell computers with my son. Do you have children?

Maria: Yes, we have a son and a daughter. They both go to school. Grandma is taking care of them now. I'm sure they are waiting for us at the airport.

Ana: Look! We're landing.

VOCABULARY

avionul	airplane	tocmai	just
a trecut	has passed	granița	border
română	Romanian	două	two
cupluri	couples	stau	sit
pe	on	același	same
rând	row	doamna	Madame, Mrs.
au căzut	have fallen	ochelarii	glasses
sunteți	you are	foarte	very
amabil	kind, nice	știți	(you) know
la	at	ce	what
ora	hour	aterizăm	(we) land
da	yes	unu	one
și	and	jumătate	half
e,este	is	soția	wife
mea	my	dintru	from
ne întoarcem	(we) come back	o	a,an
priviți	look	excursie	trip
în	in	suntem	(we) are
din	from	eu	I
sunt	am	aceasta	this
români	Romanians	cu	with
dar	but	am plecat	(we) have left
acum	now	cincisprezece	fifteen
ani	years	pentru	for
prima	first	oară	time
că	that	venim	(we) come
înapoi	back	pot	may (I)
să întreb	ask	lucrați	(you) work
profesoara	teacher	doctor	doctor
dumneavoastră	you	bancă	bank
fiul	son	meu	my
calculatoare	computers	aveți	(you) have
copii	children	fiică	daughter
merg	(they) go	amândoi	both
școala	school	acum	now
bunica	grandmother	are grijă	take care
ei	they	precis	by all means
ne așteaptă	(they) wait	aeroport	airport

EXPRESSIONS

scuzați(-mă)	excuse me
poftiți	please, here you are
vă rog	please
mulțumesc (frumos)	thank you (very much)
sunteți foarte amabil	you are very kind
dați-mi voie să mă prezint	let me introduce myself
dați-mi voie să vă prezint pe...	let me introduce you to..
bună dimineața	good morning
bună ziua	good afternoon
bună seara	good evening
noapte bună	good night

GRAMMAR

A. NOUNS-GENDERS

- There are three genders in Romanian:
    - Masculine - m.   an / year, bărbat / man
    - Feminine - f.   banca / bank, fiica / daughter
    - Neuter - n.   avion / airplane, rând / row

- Male beings are generally m. female beings are f., but abstract concepts and objects could be m., f. or n.

B. PRONOUNS

1. Personal Pronouns

	Singular	Plural
1-st person	**eu** - I	**noi** - we
2-nd person	**tu** - you **dumneata**	**voi** - you
3-rd person		
masculine	**el** - he **dânsul** **dumnealui**	**ei** - they **dânşii** **dumnealor**
feminine	**ea** - she **dânsa** **dumneaei**	**ele** - they **dânsele** **dumnealor**

Note:
1. Animal and objects will not be referred to by the personal pronoun. If the noun designating an animal or an object is the subject it will be omitted or just repeated.
2. **Tu** is the informal way of addressing somebody.
3. There are forms which express an intermediate level of politeness, implying a certain familiarity with the person referred to: "**dumneata**" for the second person singular and "**dânsul, dânşii, dumnealui, dumnealor, dânsa, dânsele, dumneaei, dumnealor,**" for the third person.
4. Pronouns are used infrequently in Romanian because the conjugation of the verb shows who is performing the action.

2. The Polite Form of the Personal Pronoun

2-nd person   **dumneavoastră**   you
singular / plural

Note:
1. The polite form of the personal pronoun is abbreviated to **dvs.** or **d-voastră**.

2. It is always used with the verb in the second person plural, even if addressing a single person.

C. VERBS

The present tense of the verb **a fi** (to be)

Affirmative

eu	sunt	I am
tu	ești	you are
el/ea	este, e	s/he is
noi	suntem	we are
voi	sunteți	you are
ei/ele	sunt	they are

Negative

eu	nu sunt	I am not
tu	nu ești	you are not
el/ea	nu este,e	s/he is not
noi	nu suntem	we are not
voi	nu sunteți	you are not
ei/ele	nu sunt	they are not

Interrogative

sunt	eu ?	am I ?
ești	tu ?	are you ?
este,e	el/ea ?	is s/he
suntem	noi ?	are we ?
sunteți	voi ?	are you ?
sunt	ei/ele ?	are they?

- in the 3-rd person singular there are two forms **este** and **e**, identical in meaning.

EXERCISES

1. Read the Romanian text aloud several times.

2. Practice how to introduce yourself or a friend.

3. Fill the correct form of the verb "to be."
   Eu..... româncă. Ce.... tu? Ea nu.... doctoriță.

39

L E C Ţ I A D O I

LA VAMĂ

Sosirea în Bucureşti

La paşapoarte

Radu: Domnule Ionescu, vă puteţi lua bagajele de acolo şi controlul paşapoartelor e aici.

Mihai: Mulţumesc frumos.

Ofiţerul: Bună ziua, pot să văd paşapoartele dumneavoastră, vă rog? Aveţi nume româneşti. Vorbiţi româneşte?

Mihai: Desigur. suntem născuţi aici.

Ofiţerul: Cât rămineţi aici şi unde mergeţi?

Ana: Vrem să stăm două săptămâni şi vom sta la hotelul Intercontinental.

Ofiţerul: Vă mulţumesc. Controlul vamal este în stânga.

La vamă.

Ofiţerul: Bună ziua. Aveţi ceva de declarat?

Mihai: Nu. Am adus doar mici cadouri.

Ofiţerul: Aş dori să văd acest bagaj. Vreţi să-l deschideţi, vă rog?

Mihai: Sigur. Poftiţi, vă rog.

Ofiţerul: Totul e în regula, vă mulţumesc. Vă doresc o vacanţă plăcută. La revedere.

LESSON TWO

CUSTOMS

Arriving in Bucharest

Passport Checkpoint (Immigration)

Radu: Mr.Ionescu you can pick up your luggage there and here is the passport checkpoint.

Mihai: Thank you.

Officer: Good afternoon, may I see your passports? You have Romanian names. Do you speak Romanian?

Mihai: Of course, we were born here.

Officer: How long will you be here and where will you be staying?

Ana: We want to stay two weeks and we'll stay at the Intercontinental Hotel.

Officer: Thank you very much. Customs is at your left.

Customs

Officer: Good afternoon. Do you have anything to declare?

Mihai: No, we brought only small gifts.

Officer: I'd like to see this suitcase. Could you open it for me, please?

Mihai: Of course, here you are.

Officer: Everything is all right, thank you. Have a nice vacation here! Good bye!

VOCABULARY

puteți	(you) can	lua	take
bagajele	luggage	de	of, from
acolo	there	controlul	control
pașapoarte	passports	aici	here
să văd	(I) see	nume	names
românești	Romanian	vorbiți	(you) speak
născuți	born	cât	how (long)
rămâneți	(you) stay	unde	where
mergeți	(you) go	vrem	(we) want
să stăm	(we) stay	două	two
săptămâni	weeks	vamal	customs
stânga	left	ceva	anything
declarat	declared	am adus	(we) brought
doar	only	mici	small
cadouri	gifts	aș dori	I would like
acest	this	vreți	you want (would you)
deschideți	open	sigur	sure
totul	everything	în regulă	all right
vă doresc	I wish	vacanță	holiday
plăcută	nice		

EXPRESSIONS

aveți ceva de declarat?	do you have anything to declare?
vacanță plăcută!	have a nice vacation!
controlul pașapoartelor	passport control
stânga	left
dreapta	right
înainte	ahead, in front
înapoi	back, backwards
lateral	sideways, laterally

GRAMMAR

A. THE ARTICLE

The characteristic feature of the definite article is the postposition, while the indefinite article is placed always before the noun.

1. The Indefinite Article

	Masculine, Neuter	Feminine
singular	un - an, a	o - an, a
plural	Masc. Fem. Neuter	
	nişte - some	

Examples:
un fiu - nişte fii; o fiică - nişte fiice;
un avion - nişte avioane

B. THE NOUN

1. The Plural with Indefinite Article

Nouns might take various ends to form the plural.
Generally, masculine nouns take the ending **-i**, feminine nouns take the ending **-e** or **-i**, neuter nouns take the ending **-e** or **-uri**.
Many nouns undergo various phonetic changes.

Masculine

Masculine nouns ending in -t change it into -ţ when the ending -i is added or the *final vowel* might be replaced by the inflection -i:

| un student | nişte studenţi - some students |
| un metru | nişte metri - some meters |

Feminine

a. Feminine nouns ending in -ă change it in -i or in -e:

| o bibliotecă | nişte biblioteci | - some bookcases |
| o apă | nişte ape | - some waters |

b. Feminine nouns ending in -e change it in -i and those ending in -ură take -uri :

| o femeie | nişte femei | - some women |
| o prăjitură | nişte prăjituri | - some cakes |

c. Feminine nouns ending in *-ea* or in stressed *-i* or *-a* take **-le**:

    o cafea   nişte cafe**le**   - some coffees
    o măsea   nişte mase**le**   - some teeth
    o zi   nişte zi**le**   - some days
    o pijama   nişte pijama**le**   - some pajamas

Neuter

a. Neuter nouns ending in *-u* change it in **-e**. The ones ending in a *consonant* add the inflection **-e**:

    un teatru   nişte teatr**e**   - some theaters
    un scaun   nişte scaun**e**   - some chairs

b. Neuter nouns ending in a *consonant* or a *vowel* may add the inflection **-uri**:

    un tren   nişte tren**uri**   - some trains
    un stilou   nişte stil**ouri** - some pens

2. The Plural with Definite Article

a. The article **-i** is added to the plural form of masculine nouns.

    nişte pomi (some trees)   pomi**i** (the trees)
    nişte pereţi (some walls)   pereţi**i** (the walls)

b. The article **-le** is added to the plural form of feminine and neuter nouns.

Feminine:

    nişte camere (some rooms)   camere**le** (the rooms)
    nişte zile (some days)   zile**le** (the days)
    nişte păpuşi (some dolls)   păpuşi**le** (the dolls)

Neuter:

    nişte teatre (some theaters)   teatre**le** (the theaters)
    nişte scaune (some chairs)   scaune**le** (the chairs)

C. THE VERB

The present tense of the verb **a avea** (to have)

Affirmative

eu	am	I have
tu	ai	you have
el/ea	are	s/he has
noi	avem	we have
voi	aveți	you have
ei/ele	au	they have

Negative

eu nu am	I do not
tu nu ai	you do not
el/ea nu are	s/he do not
noi nu avem	we do not
voi nu aveți	you do not
ei/ele nu au	they do not

Interrogative

am eu?	Do I have?
ai tu?	Do you have?
are el/ea?	Does s/he have?
avem noi?	Do we have?
aveți voi?	So you have?
au ei/ele?	Do they have?

EXERCISES

1. Read the Romanian text aloud several times.

2. Write the plural of the following nouns:
avion, ochelari, doctor, fiica, copil, bagaj, pașaport, săptămâna, cadou.

3. Fill in the correct form of the verb "to have."
(2-nd person plural)..... multe bagaje? Noi.... puține cadouri. Ele nu.... copii.... tu un pașaport?

L E C Ț I A T R E I

TRANSPORTURI LOCALE

Taxi

Familia Popescu s-a întâlnit cu copiii și bunica la ieșire.

Fiica: Cum a fost zborul, mamă?

Maria: Totul a fost perfect. Am făcut cunoștință cu o familie foarte simpatică în avion. Îi veți cunoaște în curând căci i-am invitat la cină săptămâna viitoare.

Radu: Haideți! Hai să mergem acasă. Uite un taxi!

Șoferul: Bună ziua! Unde vreți să mergeți?

Radu: Strada Eminescu, numărul 20. Știți unde e?

Șoferul: Da. În centru. Dar, cred că mai aveți nevoie de o mașină. Aveți foarte multe bagaje și nu e permis să transport cinci persoane într-o mașină.

Radu: Bine. Maria, du-te tu cu copiii. Ne vedem acasa.

....

Radu: Am avut noroc, nu a fost prea mult trafic. Vă rog să opriți acolo. Aceea este casa noastră. Cât costă?

Șoferul: Aparatul de taxat arată 525 de lei.

Radu: Poftiți 600 de lei și puteți păstra restul. Îmi puteți da o chitanță, vă rog?

Șoferul: Da, poftiți și mulțumesc.

Radu: Mulțumesc. La revedere.

L E S S O N   T H R E E

LOCAL TRANSPORTATION

Taxi

The Popescus met their children and their grandmother at the exit.

Girl: How was your flight, mother?

Maria: Everything was perfect. We met a really nice couple on the airplane. You'll see them soon because we invited them for dinner next week.

Radu: Come on ! Let's go home. Here is a taxi.

Driver: Good afternoon, where would you like to go?

Radu: 20 Eminescu Street. Do you know where it is?

Driver: Yes, downtown. But I think you'll need another taxi. You have too much luggage and I'm not allowed to carry five people in one car.

Radu: It's all right. Maria, you go with the children. I'll see you at home.

....

Radu: We were lucky, the traffic wasn't heavy. Please stop here. This is our house. How much is it?

Driver: The meter shows 525 lei.

Radu: Here you are, 600 lei and please keep the change. Would you give me a receipt, please?

Driver: Yes. Here you are and thank you.

Radu: Thank you. Good bye!

VOCABULARY

a întâlnit	have met	ieşire	exit
cum	how	a fost	(it) was
zborul	flight	perfect	perfect
familie	family	simpatică	nice
îi	them	veţi cunoaşte	will meet
curând	soon	căci	because
am invitat	(we) invited	cina	dinner
viitoare	next	acasă	home
uite	look	un	a, an
unde	where	vreţi	(you) want
să mergeţi	(you) go	strada	street
numărul	number	ştiţi	(you) know
centru	downtown	cred	(I) think
nevoie	need	maşina	car
multe	many	permis	permitted
să transport	to carry	cinci	five
persoane	persons	întru	in
bine	O.K.	du(-te)	(you) go
ne	us	vedem	(we) see
prea	too	trafic	traffic
să opriţi	to stop	aceea	that
casa	house	noastră	our
arată	(it) shows	puteţi	(you) can
păstra	to keep	restul	change
da	to give	chitanţă	receipt

EXPRESSIONS

a face cunoştinţă cu...	to meet...
	to make somebody's acquaintance
haideţi!	come on!
hai să mergem	let's go
unde vreţi să mergeţi?	where do you want to go?
a avea nevoie de	to need...
a avea noroc	to be lucky
cât costă?	how much does it cost?
aparat de taxat	meter
puteţi păstra restul	you can keep the change
aveţi mărunt?	do you have change?

GRAMMAR

1. THE ARTICLE

THE POSSESSIVE ARTICLE

	masculine	feminine	neuter
singular	**al**	**a**	**al**
plural	**ai**	**ale**	**ale**

Note:
1. The possessive article always agrees in gender and number with the object possessed.

2. It is used in genitive constructions.

3. The possessive article is placed before:
   - a noun in the Genitive, when the noun has no definite article.

   *Este un bagaj **al** soţiei mele.*

but when the noun has the definite article:

   Este bagaj<u>ul</u> soţiei mele.

   - a possessive adjective, if the noun it determines has no definite article.

   *Iau un bagaj **al** tău.*

but with definite article

   Iau bagaj<u>ul</u> tău.

2. PERSONAL PRONOUN - GENITIVE

	singular		plural
	masculine	feminine	masculine, feminine
(al, a, ai, ale)	**lui**	**ei**	**lor**
	his	hers	theirs

Note:

1. The personal pronoun has Genitive forms only in the 3-rd. person sg. and pl.. For the other persons the genitival relation is expressed by the corresponding possessive pronouns and adjectives.

2. The Genitive forms will be preceded by the Possessive Article.

Cartea este **a** lui. / The book is his./
Bagajele sunt **ale** lor. / The baggage are theirs./

3. NOUNS

a. Declension with Indefinite Article

	singular	plural
Masculine		
Nom.Acc.	**un** pom	**nişte** pomi
Gen.Dat.	**unui** pom	**unor** pomi
Feminine		
Nom.Acc.	**o** floare	**nişte** flori
Gen.Dat.	**unei** flori	**unor** flori
Neuter		
Nom.Acc.	**un** caiet	**nişte** caiete
Gen.Dat.	**unui** caiet	**unor** caiete

Note:

1. Masculine and neuter nouns have the same form throughout all four cases singular and another throughout the four cases plural.

2. Feminine nouns have one form for Nominative and Accusative singular and one form for Genitive and Dative singular. For plural, feminine nouns have the same form throughout the four cases.

4. ADVERBS

a. Interrogative and Relative Adverbs

The adverbs: **unde** (where), **cum** (how), **când** (when) are used in:

- independent or main clauses as interrogative adverbs

Unde mergeţi?   **Where** are you going?
Cum îţi/vă place?   **How** do you like it?
Când plecăm?   **When** do we leave?

- subordinate clauses as relative adverbs

Merge **unde** îi place.   He goes **where** he likes.
Nu ştie **cum** îi va place.   He doesn't know **how** she'll like it.
Va telefona **când** va ajunge. He will call **when** he arrives.

B. **ADVERBS OF PLACE**

The most frequently used adverbs of place are:

aici	(here)	acolo	(there)
sus	(up)	jos	(down)
aprpape	(near)	departe	(far)
afara	(outside)	inauntru	(inside)

C. **ADVERBS OF TIME**

The most frequently used adverbs of time are:

azi	(today)	maine	(tomorrow)
acum	(now)	atunci	(then)
devreme	(early)	tarziu	(late)
ieri	(yesterday)		

EXERCISES

1. Try to memorize the text.

2. Complete the blanks with the possessive article:

    Copilul acesta este.... meu iar fetiţa este... lui.
    Ochelarii sunt... dumneavoastră, iar ziarele sunt...
    mele. Florile sunt... doamnei de acolo.

3. Complete the blanks with the adequate adverbs:

    Nu ştie... să meargă la adresa aceasta.
    A întrebat... soseşte avionul la aeroport.

L E C Ț I A P A T R U

LA HOTEL

Familia Ionescu tocmai a ajuns la hotelul Intercontinental.

Mihai: Bună ziua. Numele meu e Ionescu Mihai. Am rezervată din New York o cameră pentru două persoane.

Recep-
ționistul: Da, domnule. Vă rog să completați aceste formulare... Mulțumesc. Aveți camera 312, care e la etajul trei. Ascensorul e la dreapta, lângă scări. Aceasta e cheia. Bagajele vor fi aduse în cameră imediat.

Mihai: Mulțumesc. Unde putem parca mașina, vă rog?

Recep-
ționistul: În parcarea hotelului care e la subsol.

Ana: Puteți să-mi spuneți, vă rog, unde și la ce oră putem lua micul dejun? Am înțeles că este inclus în preț.

Recep-
ționistul: Restaurantul este acolo, față în față cu barul. Puteți lua micul dejun acolo, între orele 7 și 10 dimineața. Dar puteți cere să vă fie servit în cameră.

Ana: Ce alte servicii mai oferiți?

Recep-
ționistul: Hotelul are un coafor, poștă, un magazin cu cadouri și un birou de schimb valutar aici la parter. Bazinul de înot și sala de sport sunt la subsol. Dacă mai aveți nevoie de ceva, vă stăm la dispoziție.

LESSON FOUR

HOTEL

Mr. and Mrs. Ionescu arrive at the Intercontinental Hotel.

Mihai: Good afternoon. My name is Ionescu Mihai. I reserved a room for two from New York.

Clerk: Yes, Sir. Please fill out these forms... Thank you. Your room number is 312 and it is on the third floor. The elevator is on the right, next to the stairs. The baggage will be brought to your room immediately.

Mihai: Thanks. Where can we park the car, please?

Clerk: In the hotel's underground parking lot.

Ana: Could you tell me when and where we can have breakfast? I understood it's included in the price.

Clerk: The restaurant is opposite the bar. You can have breakfast there from 7:00am-10:00am. But you can ask for room service too.

Ana: What other kind of services do you offer?

Clerk: Here on the first floor we have a hair dresser, a post office, a gift shop and a currency exchange. The swimming pool and the health club are in the basement. If you need anything else, please let us know.

VOCABULARY

a ajuns	they got	numele	name
meu	mine	am rezervată	I reserved
camera	room	două	two
aceste	this	etajul	floor
trei	three	ascensor	elevator
lângă	near	scări	stairs
cheia	key	imediat	immediately
a parca	to park	parcare	parking lot
care	which	subsol	underground
am înțeles	I understood	inclus	included
preț	price	acolo	there
cere	to ask	ce	what
alte	others	oferiți	you offer
coafor	hairdresser	poșta	post office
aici	here	parter	ground level

EXPRESSIONS

am rezervată o cameră	I reserved a room
a completa formulare	to fill out forms
puteți să-mi spuneți	could you tell me..
a lua micul dejun	to have breakfast
a servi prânzul, cina	to have lunch, dinner
la ce oră?	what time?
față în față	across from each other
magazin cu cadouri	gift shop
birou de schimb valutar	currency exchange office
bazin de înot	swimming pool
sala de sport	health club
aveți nevoie de ceva?	do you need anything else?
vă stăm la dispoziție	let us know

GRAMMAR

A. PERSONAL PRONOUN

1. The Dative Forms

	Singular	Plural
1-st person	**mie** - me	**nouă** - us
unstressed form	**îmi**,-mi-	-ne, -ni-
2-nd person	**ţie** - you	**vouă** - you
unstressed form	**îţi**,-ţi-	**vă**,vi,v-

3-rd person   masculine   feminine   masculine   feminine

        lui - him **ei** - her   **lor** - them **lor** - them

unstressed form îi,-i- îi,-i   -le-,li -le-,li

Note:

1. The personal pronoun has two forms for the Dative: the stressed form and the unstressed form.

2. The stressed forms of the Dative are used with the corresponding unstressed Dative and are used without any preposition.

Example:

    Ţie *îţi* dau cartea.   I am giving you the book.
    Ei *îi* spun o poveste.   I am telling her a story.

3. The Dative of personal pronouns is used with common expressions. In this case it will join the word which precedes or follows the pronoun, when this word ends or begins with a vowel:

    a-i părea bine   to be glad
    Mie *îmi* pare bine că plec.
    Îmi pare bine că plec.   I'm glad I'm leaving.

    a-i fi sete   to be thirsty
    Ţie *îţi* e sete.
    Ţi-e sete.   you are thirsty.

    a-i fi foame   to be hungry
    Vouă *vă* e foame?
    Vi-e foame?   Are you hungry?

a-i fi cald	to be warm
Ei (Lui) *îi* este cald.	
I-e cald.	She is warm.
a-i fi frig	to be cold
a-i fi somn	to be sleepy
a-i părea rău	to be sorry

The Dative is used with the verb **"a trebui"** in the sense of "to need" and with the verb **"a plăcea"** meaning "to like, to love."

Example:

(Lui) *îi* trebuie un bilet.	He needs a ticket.
(Nouă) *Ne* trebuie hârtie.	We need paper.
(Lui) *Îi* place de Ileana.	He likes Ileana.
(Tie) *Îți* plac poveștile?	Do you like stories?

2. THE CARDINAL NUMERAL

1	unu	6	șase
2	doi	7	șapte
3	trei	8	opt
4	patru	9	nouă
5	cinci	10	zece

Note:

1. Before a noun, the cardinal numerals **un** and **doi** have different forms each, according to the gender of the noun.

   masculine **un** copil - one child **doi** copii - two children

   feminine **o** fetiță - a girl **două** fetițe - two girls

2. To form 11 -19, the word **"sprezece"** is used, being preceded by the cardinal numerals expressing the units.

11	un**sprezece**	16	șai**sprezece**
12	doi**sprezece**	17	șapte**sprezece**
13	trei**sprezece**	18	opt**sprezece**
14	pai**sprezece**	19	nouă**sprezece**
15	cinci**sprezece**		

3. To form 20-90, the word **"zeci"** is used, being preceded by the unit indicating the tens.

20	două**zeci**	60	şai**zeci**
30	trei**zeci**	70	şapte**zeci**
40	patru**zeci**	80	opt**zeci**
50	cinci**zeci**	90	nouă**zeci**

To form 100 and more just enumerate the units starting with the largest ones:

100	o sută	2,000	două mii
200	două sute	10,000	zece mii
1000	o mie	one million	un milion

Example:

1.245 - o mie două sute patruzeci şi cinci

The full stop **(.)** is used to separate the thousands and a comma /virgula/ **(,)** is the equivalent of the decimal point in English:

English	Romanian	
2.3	2,3	(decimal point)
4.53	4,53	
1,200	1.200	(separates thousands)
14,500	14.500	

EXERCISES

1. Try to memorize the text.

2. Fill in the correct forms of the stressed and/or unstressed personal pronoun:

(III.pl.f.)-am dat cărţile prietenilor mei. (I.sg.) place de Maria. (II.pl.) e foame? (III.sg.m.) trebuie maşina azi de după-masă.

3. Translate into Romanian:

I like this room. We visited 11 towns. They reserved room number 582. You (II.pl.) may take the bus number 34 to the hotel.

LECȚIA CINCI

LA PLIMBARE

Familia Ionescu a plecat la plimbare.

Ana: Scuzați-mă, puteți să-mi spuneți unde e poșta, vă rog?

Domnul: Mergeți până la primul stop, acolo o luați la stânga și la al doilea colț la dreapta. Poșta e a treia clădire pe partea stângă. Puteți merge pe jos, dar puteți lua și troleibuzul 34. Prima stație e muzeul iar a doua e opera. Vă dați jos acolo și poșta e în spatele operei.

Ana: Mulțumesc.

La poștă.

Mihai: Bună dimineața. Aș dori să trimit aceste scrisori în Statele Unite.

Funcționar 1: La al treilea ghișeu, vă rog. Aici e pentru pachete.

Mihai: Cât costă să trimit aceste scrisori, par avion, la New York?

Funcționar 2: Trebuie să le cântăresc mai întâi... costă o sută șaisprezece lei de scrisoare.

Mihai: În cât timp o să ajungă acolo?

Funcționar 2: Aproximativ într-o săptămână.

Mihai: Mulțumesc. La revedere.

LESSON FIVE

GOING FOR A WALK

ASKING FOR DIRECTIONS

The Ionescus went for a walk.

Ana: Excuse me, could you tell me where the post office is?

Gentleman: Go straight down this street until the first light. Turn to the left and at the second corner turn right. The post office is the third building on the left side. You can walk there but you can also use the trolley bus number 34. The first stop is the museum. The second is the Opera. Get off there and the post office is behind the Opera.

Ana: Thank you.

At the post office.

Mihai: Good morning. I'd like to send these letters to America.

Clerk 1: Please go to the third window. This one is just for packages.

Mihai: How much does it cost to send these letters by airmail to New York?

Clerk 2: I have to weigh them first... it will be 116 lei for each letter.

Mihai: How long does it take for them to get there?

Clerk 2: About one week.

Mihai: Thank you. Good bye.

VOCABULARY

primul	the first	stop	traffic light
al doilea	the second	colţ	corner
a treia	the third	clădire	building
parte	side	a lua	to take
troleibuz	trolley bus	staţie	stop, station
aş dori	I would	să trimit	to send
scrisori	letters	ghişeu	counter
pachete	packages	trebuie	I must
să cântăresc	to weigh	mai întii	first
săptămâna	week		

EXPRESSIONS

a merge la plimbare	to take a walk
o luaţi la stânga...	take a left...
faceţi dreapta...	take a right
în faţă	across
în spatele	behind
mergeţi trei colţuri...	go straight three blocks
a merge pe jos	to walk
a se da jos	to get off
cât costă?	how much does it cost?
cât face?	how much does it cost?
în cât timp?	how long?
timbru	stamp
par avion	by airmail

GRAMMAR

1. DECLENSION WITH DEFINITE ARTICLE

	masculine	neuter	feminine
Nom.Acc. Singular	-(u)u; -le	-(u)l; -le	-(u)a
Gen.Dat. Singular	-(u)lui	-(u)lui	-i
Nom.Acc. Plural	-i	-i, -le	-le
Gen.Dat. Plural	-lor	-lor	-lor

Note:

1. The characteristic feature of the definite article is the post-position.

2. Singular

a. The article **-ul** is added to nouns (m. or n.) ending in **-i** or in a **consonant**.

    un tramvai (a tram)   tramvaiul (the tram)
    un pom (a tree)   pomul (the tree)

b. The article **-l** is added to nouns (m. or n.) ending in **-u**.

    un teatru (a theater)   teatrul (the theater)

c. The article **-le** is added to nouns (m. or n.) ending in **-e**.

    un perete (a wall)   peretele (the wall)

d. The article **-ua** is added to nouns (f.) ending in **a vowel**.

    o zi (a day)   ziua (the day)
    o lalea (a tulip)   laleaua (the tulip)

e. The article **-a** is added to nouns (f.) ending in **-e**.

    o carte (a book)   cartea (the book)
    o rochie (a dress)   rochia (the dress)

f. The article **-a** replaces the final vowel of nouns ending in **-a**.

   o cameră (a room)   camera (the room)

3. In the Genitive and Dative singular the Definite Article has the following forms:

a.   **-ului** for masculine and neuter nouns ending in a **consonant** or in **-i**:

    unui student   student**ului**
    unui tramvai   tramvai**ului**
    unui pom   pom**ului**

b.   **-lui** is added to all other masculine and neuter nouns:

    unui teatru   teatru**lui**
    unui perete   perete**lui**

c.   **-i** for feminine nouns:

    unei flori   flori**i**
    unei fete   fete**i**
    unei cărți   cărți**i**

4. Plural

To form the Genitive and Dative plural the termination **-lor** is added to all nouns.

    unor pomi   pomi**lor**
    unor caiete   caiete**lor**
    unor teatre   teatre**lor**
    unor femei   femei**lor**
    unor fete   fete**lor**

5.   The article **lui** may be placed before proper nouns in the Dative case.

    lui Ion   **lui** Irinel
    lui Vasile   **lui** Lulu

EXERCISES

1. Practice giving directions.

2. Translate:

The letter's stamp costs 116 lei. I give a book to Maria.
The post office is behind the opera. The baggage is my wife's.
The flowers of the women are beautiful.

LECŢIA ŞASE

LA RESTAURANT

Radu: Bună seara. Avem rezervată o masă pentru patru persoane pe numele de Popescu.

Chelner: Bună seara. Vă rog să mă urmaţi. Vă convine la această masă?

Radu: Îmi pare rău, dar cred că e prea aproape de orchestră. Ne place muzica populară, dar cred că va fi prea tare pentru conversaţia noastră.

Chelner: Este mai bine în acest colţ liniştit?

Radu: Da, mulţumesc.

Chelner: Ce aţi dori să beţi?

Maria: Aş dori un Martini sec.

Ana: Şi pentru mine la fel, vă rog.

Radu: Domnule Ionescu, nu aţi vrea să încercaţi o băutură românească? Vreţi să beţi o ţuică cu mine?

Mihai: Sigur. De ce nu?

Chelner: Aici e meniul. Vă aduc imediat şi băuturile.

Maria: Mulţumim. Doamnă Ionescu şi domnule Ionescu, hai să nu mai fim aşa formali. Spuneţi-ne Maria şi Radu, vă rog. Hai să bem "per tu."

Ana: Sigur, e mai plăcut aşa între prieteni. Noroc!

Toţi: Noroc!

Chelner: Doriţi să comandaţi?

Maria: Da. Aş dori nişte mititei cu usturoi, friptură de porc cu cartofi prăjiţi, salată de varză acră şi papanaşi cu brânză.

Ana: Pentru mine: caşcaval la capac şi tocană.

Radu: Un platou rece pentru două persoane şi pui la ceaun cu mămăligă, vă rog.

Mihai: Sărmăluţe cu smântână şi îngheţată de ciocolată, vă rog.

Chelner: Pot să vă recomand din vinurile renumitelor noastre podgorii? Merlot de Dealul Mare sau Riesling de Târnave sunt vinuri seci. Pinot Gris de Murfatlar e mai dulce.

Radu: Aduceţi-ne Merlot, vă rog.

Chelnerul aduce mâncarea şi cei patru prieteni încep să mănânce.

Radu: Cum vă simţiţi din nou în ţară?

Ana: Ne simţim foarte bine. Bucureştiul s-a schimbat mult. Ne-a fost greu să recunoaştem unele locuri.

Mihai: Am văzut multe lucruri frumoase în plimbările noastre. Nu ne place să conducem maşina aici fiindcă e aşa greu să găsim parcare şi e foarte aglomerat.

Maria: De aceea şi nouă ne place să mergem cu tramvaiul sau cu metroul. Nu conducem decât dacă mergem undeva la sfârşit de săptămână.

Chelner: V-a plăcut ce aţi servit?

Ana: Totul a fost delicios!

Chelner: Doriţi ceva desert sau cafea?

Radu: Nu, mulţumim. Nota de plată, vă rog.

Chelnerul aduce nota de plată. Radu plăteşte şi adaugă bacşişul.

LESSON SIX

AT THE RESTAURANT

Mihai: Good evening! We have reservations for four under the name of Popescu.

Waiter: Good evening, Sir! Please, follow me! Would this table be all right for you?

Mihai: I am sorry, but it is too close to the music. I like folk music, but I'm afraid it will be too loud for our conversation.

Waiter: Is this quiet corner O.K. for you?

Mihai: Yes, thank you!

Waiter: What would you like to drink?

Maria: I'd like a dry Martini.

Ana: I'll have one too.

Radu: Mr. Ionescu, would you like to try a Romanian drink? I will have țuica. Would you care to join me?

Mihai: Sure, why not!

Waiter: Here are the menus. I will bring your drinks in a moment.

Maria: Thank you. Mr. and Mrs. Ionescu, let's not be so formal any more. Why don't you call us Maria and Mihai ? Let's drink to that!

Ana: Of course, it's more pleasant among friends. Cheers!

All: Cheers!

Waiter: Are you ready to order?

Maria: Yes, I'd like sausages with garlic, a pork steak with fries, sauerkraut salad and soft little doughnut with cheese.

Ana: Breaded cheese and meat with vegetables, please.

Radu: Cold cut for two and chicken with polenta, please.

Mihai: Stuffed sauerkraut with sour cream and chocolate ice cream for me please.

Waiter: May I suggest some of our famous Romanian wines for your dinners? "Dealul Mare" Merlot or "Târnave" Riesling are dry wines, while "Murfatlar" Pinot Gris is a sweeter one.

Mihai: We'll have the Merlot, please.

Waiter: Thank you.

The food arrives and the four friends start to eat.

Radu: Are you enjoying your visit here?

Ana: Very much! Bucharest changed a lot. We could hardly recognize some places.

Mihai: We saw beautiful things on our walks. We don't like to drive here because it's so difficult to find a place to park and traffic is so heavy.

Maria: That's why we like to use the subway and the tram. We drive only if we leave town on weekends.

Waiter: Was everything all right?

Mihai: It was delicious!

Waiter: Would you like some desert or coffee?

Mihai: No, thank you, just the check, please.

The waiter brings the bill. Radu pays it and adds the tip.

VOCABULARY

să urmați	follow me	vă convine	do you like
cred	I think	prea	too
aproape	close, near	orchestra	orchestra
vă fi	it will be	tare	loud
mai bine	better	liniștit	quiet
să beți	to drink	la fel	same
ați vrea	would you like	să încercați	to try
băutură	drink	meniu	menu
recomand	to recommend	vin	wine
renumit	famous	podgorii	vineyard
mâncare	meals	prieteni	friends
din nou	again	țara	land, homeland
a schimbat	changed	mult	a lot
să recunoaștem	to recognize	unele	some
locuri	places	am văzut	we saw
multe	many	lucruri	things
frumoase	beautiful	fiindcă	because
greu	difficult	să găsim	to find
de aceea	that's why	undeva	somewhere
totul	everything	delicios	delicious
chelner	waiter	plătește	he pays

EXPRESSIONS

am rezervat o masă	we reserved a table
îmi pare rău	I am sorry
muzică populară	folk music
ce ați dori...?	what would you like to (order)
aș dori	I would like to have
de ce nu!	why not!
hai să nu mai fim așa formali	let's not be so formal anymore
noroc!	cheers!
doriți să comandați?	what would you care to order?
pot să vă recomand...	may I suggest you...
vin dulce	sweet wine
vin sec	dry wine
cum vă simțiți în excursie?	how do you like your trip?
ne-a fost greu	it was difficult
să conducem mașina	to drive the car
e aglomerat	the traffic is heavy
sfârșit de săptămână	weekend
vă place?	do you like?
nota de plată!	the bill (check please!)
bacșiș	tip

GRAMMAR

1. THE VERB

The Infinitive

According to the endings of the Infinitive of the verbs there are four conjugations:

Conjugation	Termination	Examples
1-st	-a	a lucra (to work), a spăla (to wash) a intra (to enter), a adopta (to adopt)
2-nd	- ea	a vedea (to see), a cădea (to fall) a apărea (to appear, to come out)
3-rd	- e	a merge (to go), a aduce (to bring) a naşte (to give birth)
4-th	- i,-î	a fugi (to run), a trezi (to awake) a coborî (to descend) a hotărî (to decide)

Note:

1. The infinitive is preceded by the particle **"a"** (the English "to").

2. Romanian also has the "long infinitive." It is used as a noun, defining the action expressed by the respective verb.

Example:
```
         a intra (to enter)  - intrare (entrance)
         a sosi (to arrive)  - sosire (arrival)
         a vorbi (to speak)  - vorbire (speaking)
         a adopta (to adopt) - adoptare (adoption)
```

2. PERSONAL PRONOUN ACCUSATIVE

	Singular	Plural
1-st person	**pe mine**	**pe noi**
unstressed form	**-mă, m-**	**-ne**
2-nd person	**pe tine**	**pe voi**
unstressed form	**-te-**	**-vă, v-**

3-rd person	masculine	feminine	masculine	feminine
	pe el	**pe ea**	**pe ei**	**pe ele**
unstressed form	îi, -i-	o, -o	îi, -i-	-le-

Note:

1. The personal pronoun has two forms: the stressed form and the unstressed form.

2. The stressed forms of the Accusative are used with the corresponding unstressed Accusative and are used with prepositions (pe, la, în).

Example: Pe mine mă cheamă Ileana.   My name is Ileana.
         Pe voi vă spală mama.   Mother washes you.

3. THE ADJECTIVE

Four-form Adjectives

Most Romanian Adjectives have four distinct terminations.

Singular		Plural	
masculine, neuter	feminine	masculine	feminine, neuter
-0, (-u)	**-a**	**-i**	**-e**

Note:

1. The ending **-u** occurs whenever the root of the adjective ends in a **consonant and "r" or "l"**:

   ne**gru** - black   sim**plu** - simple   am**plu** - ample

2. For some adjectives the root will remain unchanged:

    alb - white   galben - yellow   bun - good
        tipic - typical   variabil - variable

Others undergo phonetic changes:

frum**os**	frum**oasă**	- beautiful
frum**oși**	frum**oase**	
folosit**or**	folosit**oare**	- useful
folosit**ori**	folosit**oare**	

3. The adjectives will be placed after the noun and will agree in gender, number and case with it:

    o fată frum**oasă** - a beautiful girl
    un băiat frum**os** - a beautiful boy
    ale unor cărți interesant**e** - of some interesting books
    pe peretele înalt - on the high wall

EXERCISES

1. Practice how to order in restaurants.

2. Underline the Accusative forms of the Personal Pronoun in the text.

3. Translate into Romanian: Are you going to the movies? Yes, I am going. Are you taking George with you? No, I don't take George with me, I take Maria with me. We are very glad to see them. They invited us to dinner.

LECȚIA ȘAPTE

DUPĂ CUMPĂRĂTURI

Ana și Mihai vor să meargă la magazin să cumpere haine.

Ana: Grăbește-te Mihai! Magazinul se închide la ora 6 și dacă întârziem vă trebui să mergem mâine dimineață la ora 10.

Ana: Bună ziua. Vrem să cumpărăm un costum de vară pentru soțul meu.

Vânzătorul: Ce mărime, vă rog?

Mihai: 40 sau 42, nu știu exact.

Vânzătorul: Pentru aceste mărimi avem costume albe, bej și bleu.

Mihai: În gri nu aveți?

Vânzătorul: Avem dar s-ar putea să fie prea mic pentru dumneavoastră. Vreți să-l încercați? Cabina de proba e acolo.

Mihai: Mulțumesc.... E numai bun. Cât costă?

Vânzătorul: 5000 de lei.

Mihai: Poftiți. Mulțumesc. La revedere.

Ana: Ne puteți spune, vă rog, unde sunt pantofii?

Vânzătorul: Acolo, chiar în spatele dumneavoastră.

Vânzător 2: Cu ce vă pot ajuta?

Ana: Aș dori o pereche de pantofi albi, cu tocuri mărimea 38.

Vânzător 2: Puteți găsi diverse modele pe cele două rafturi de acolo.

Ana: Mulțumesc. Aș dori să cumpăr această pereche.

Vânzător 2: Îmi pare rău dar nu mai avem acest model în mărimea 38. Poate mai primim săptămâna viitoare.

Ana: Mulțumesc. Voi veni atunci.

LESSON SEVEN

SHOPPING

Ana and Mihai want to go to buy clothes.

Ana: Hurry, Mihai! The store will close at 6 p.m. and if we're late we'll have to go tomorrow at 10 a.m.

....

Ana: Good afternoon! We'd like to buy a summer suit for my husband.

Clerk: What size, please?

Mihai: 40 or 42, I'm not sure.

Clerk: In this range we have white, beige and light blue.

Mihai: Do you have them in gray, too?

Clerk: Yes, we do, but it might be too small for you. Do you want to try it? The fitting room is there.

Mihai: Thank you. It's just perfect. How much is it?

Clerk: 5,000 lei.

Mihai: Here you are. Thank you. Good bye!

....

Ana: Could you tell us where the shoe department is?

Clerk 2: There, behind you. May I help you?

Ana: I'd like a nice pair of white high-heeled shoes, size 38.

Clerk 2: You can find some samples on the two shelves over there.

Ana: Thank you. I'd like to buy this pair.

Clerk 2: I'm sorry, but we are out of these, in size 38. Maybe we'll have them next week.

Ana: Thank you. I'll come back.

VOCABULARY

magazin	shop	**să cumpere**	to buy
haine	clothes	**se închide**	closes
întârziem	we are late	**mâine**	tomorrow
soţul	husband	**pantofii**	shoes
pereche	pair	**mărimea**	size
găsi	to find	**diverse**	various
modele	samples	**rafturi**	shelves
primim	we receive	**atunci**	then

EXPRESSIONS

grăbeşte-te	hurry
costum de vară	summer suit
ce mărime?	what size?
nu ştiu exact	I don't know for sure
s-ar putea să fie mic	it might be too small
vreţi să încercaţi?	do you want to try?
cabina de probă	fitting room
e numai bun	it is just fine
cât costă?	how much is it?
cu ce vă pot ajuta?	how may I help you?
pantofi cu tocuri	high heeled shoes

Colors

alb	white	verde	green
bej	beige	albastru	blue
gri	gray	mov	purple
galben	yellow	violet	violet
roşu	red	maro	brown
portocaliu	orange	negru	black

GRAMMAR

1. THE ADJECTIVE

Three-form Adjectives have one form for masculine singular, one form for feminine singular and the same form for masculine and feminine plural.

	singular	plural
masculine	-0	-i
feminine	-a, -e	-i, -e

Note:

The three-form adjectives are:

1. Masculine singular adjectives ending in -c or -g:

```
         singular                    plural
M.   băiat mic - a little boy     băieți mici
F.   fată mica - a little girl    fete mici
N.   creion mic - a little pencil creioane mici
```

2. Adjectives ending in -iu (M. or N. sg.)

```
M.  perete cenușiu - a gray wall      pereți cenușii
F.  casă cenușie - a gray house       case cenușii
N.  avion cenușiu - a gray airplane   avioane cenușii
```

3. Adjectives ending in -esc, being used only with N. and F. nouns denoting inanimate objects:

```
o carte românească - a Romanian book    cărți românești
un roman Românesc - a Romanian novel    romane românești
```

2. THE VERB

PRESENT INDICATIVE

	Verbs ending in -a		Verbs ending in -i	
Singular				
1-st person	o,-u	-ez	-o	-esc
2-nd person	-i	-ezi	-e	-şti
3-rd person	-ă	-ează	-e	-eşte
Plural				
1-st person	-ăm	-ăm	-im	-im
2-nd person	-aţi	-a ti	-iţi	-iţi
3-rd person	-ă	-ează	-o	-esc

Note:

1. All regular verbs ending in **-A** have homonymous forms for the 3-rd person singular and plural.

   el, ei umblă; el, ei spală; el, ei lucrează

2. Verbs ending in **-I** have homonymous forms for the 3-rd person plural and 1-st person singular.

   eu, ei simt; eu, ei dorm; eu, ei citesc

3. The 1-st person singular has the ending in **-U** after all root-forms ending in consonants: "r," "l."

   eu intru, eu umblu,

4. Where there is no continuous or progressive form, the Present Indicative in Romanian corresponds to the Present Indefinite and Present Continuous in English.

5. In Romanian the Present Tense is often used with a future meaning, accompanied by an adverb of future time or alone.

   Mergem mâine la film? Will we go tomorrow to a movie?
   Îţi citesc mai târziu. I will read you later.

Examples:

Verbs ending in -A

	a căuta /to search/	a intra /to enter/	a completa /to fill out/
1.	caut	intru	completez
2.	cauţi	intri	completezi
3.	caută	intră	completează
4.	căutăm	intrăm	completăm
5.	căutaţi	intraţi	completaţi
6.	caută	intră	completează

Verbs ending in -I

	a simţi /to feel/	a acoperi /to cover/	a povesti /to tell stories/
1.	simt	acopăr	povestesc
2.	simţi	acoperi	povesteşti
3.	simte	acoperă	povesteşte
4.	simţim	acoperim	povestim
5.	simţiţi	acoperiţi	povestiţi
6.	simt	acoperă	povestesc

EXERCISES

1. Practice buying a suit and a pair of shoes.

2. Conjugate the verbs:

a cumpăra; a încerca; a vorbi; a veni

LECŢIA OPT

ÎN VIZITĂ

Ana: Maria ne-a invitat la cină astă-seară.

Mihai: Ce drăguţ din partea lor. La ce oră?

Ana: La şapte. Dar vom pleca mai devreme, pentru că ar trebui să cumpărăm un mic cadou.

Mihai: Ce vrei să cumperi?

Ana: Flori, o sticlă cu vin şi ciocolată pentru copii. Repede într-o oră plecăm.

La familia Popescu. Sună soneria.

Maria: Sunt Ana şi Mihai. Deschide tu uşa, te rog.

Radu: Bună seară. Poftiţi înăuntru. A fost greu să ne găsiţi?

Mihai: Nu, a fost uşor pentru că am luat un taxi. Poftiţi: nişte flori pentru stăpâna casei şi o sticla cu vin pentru tine. Unde sunt copiii?

Maria: Sunt la bunica. Florile sunt foarte frumoase. Mulţumesc.

Radu: Ce vreţi să beţi? Gin sau votca?

Ana: Gin cu tonic, te rugăm.

Radu: Hai să vă arăt apartamentul. Nu e mare dar e comfortabil. Aici sunt dormitoarele şi baia, şi în bucătărie se intră din sufragerie.

Mihai: Ce miroase aşa bine aici?

Maria: Am pregătit mâncare specific românească. Uite!

Ana: Dar Maria, nu putem mânca atâta. E prea mult chiar şi pentru o săptămână.

Maria: Mai vedem noi.

Dupa cină.

Mihai:	Am mâncat prea mult, dar totul a fost foarte bun. Mulțumim.
Maria:	Cu plăcere. Poftiți în sufragerie să servim o cafea.
Ana:	Lasă-mă să te ajut să strângem masa.
Maria:	Strânsul mesei mai poate să aștepte.

După două ore.

Mihai:	E foarte târziu. Trebuie să plecăm. Poți să chemi un taxi, te rog?
Radu:	Cu plăcere. (Formează numărul). Bună seara. Puteți trimite un taxi pe: strada Eminescu 20, telefon 123456? Mulțumesc. Va fi aici în zece minute.
Ana:	Vă mulțumim pentru această seară minunată. Ne-am simțit foarte bine. Maria, o să te sun mâine. La revedere.
Maria și Radu:	La revedere.

LESSON EIGHT

BEING A GUEST

Ana: The Popescu's invited us for dinner tonight.

Mihai: How nice of them. What time?

Ana: Seven o'clock. We should leave earlier, because we need to buy them a gift.

Mihai: What do you want to buy?

Ana: Flowers, a bottle of wine and some chocolate for the kids. Hurry, we have to leave in an hour.

At the Popescu's home. The bell rings.

Maria: Ana and Mihai are here. Open the door, please.

Radu: Hi! Please, come in. Was it difficult to find our place?

Mihai: No, it was easy because we took a taxi! Here are some flowers for the lady of the house and a bottle of wine for you. Where are the kids?

Maria: They are at grandma's. These flowers are beautiful, thanks.

Radu: What would you like to drink? Gin or vodka?

Ana: We'll have a gin and tonic, please.

Radu: Let me show you around. The apartment is not big but it is very comfortable. Here are the bedrooms and the bathroom, the kitchen opens off the living room.

Mihai: Something smells delicious here. What is it?

Maria: I prepared a traditional Romanian dinner. Have a look!

Ana: But, Maria, we can not eat everything. It is too much even for a week.

Maria: We'll see.

After dinner.

Mihai: I ate too much, but everything was so good. Thank you.

Maria: You're welcome. Let's go to the living room.

Ana: Let me help you clean the table.

Maria: No, thank you, this can wait.

Two hours later.

Mihai: It's very late. We must go. Could you call a taxi for us, please?

Radu: Of course. (He dials.) Good evening. Could you send a cab to: 20, Eminescu Street, telephone 123456? Thank you. It will be here in ten minutes.

Ana: Thanks for the wonderful evening. We really enjoyed your hospitality. Maria, I'll call you tomorrow. Good bye.

Maria and Radu: Bye! Good night!

VOCABULARY

a invitat	she invited	**vom pleca**	we will leave
flori	flowers	**ciocolată**	chocolate
copii	children	**repede**	hurry
sună	it rings	**soneria**	door bell
deschide	open!	**uşa**	door
să arăt	to show	**apartamentul**	apartment
mare	big	**dormitoarele**	bedrooms
baia	bathroom	**bucătărie**	kitchen
sufragerie	living-room	**miroase**	it smells
am pregătit	I prepared	**specific**	typical
atâta	so much	**prea mult**	too much
chiar	even	**târziu**	late
trimiteţi	you send	**minunată**	wonderful
să sun	I will call		

EXPRESSIONS

astă-seară	this evening
ce drăguţ din partea lor	how nice of them
la ce oră?	what time?
sticlă cu vin	a bottle of wine
poftiţi înăuntru	please come in
a fost greu?	was it difficult...?
a fost uşor	it was easy...
stăpâna casei	the lady of the house
hai	let's
mai vedem noi (informal)	we'll see
lasă-mă să te ajut	let me help you
să strângem masa	let's clear the table
să punem masa	let's set the table
a chema un taxi	to call a cab
formează numărul	he dials
o să te sun	I'll call you

GRAMMAR

1. ADJECTIVES

Comparative Degree

Superiority	**mai** more	+ adjective + **decât** than

Equality	**tot aşa** **la fel** as	**de** + adjective + **ca** as

Inferiority	**mai puţin** + adjective + **decît**
	less than

Examples:

Maria este **mai frumoasa decât** Ana.
Mary is more beautiful than Ana.

Maşina roşie este **tot aşa de rapidă ca** şi maşina albă.
The red car is as fast as the white car.

Lecţia 8 e **mai puţin dificilă decât** lecţia 7.
Lesson 8 is less difficult than lesson 7.

Superlative Degree

Relative	Superiority **cel, cea mai** +adj. (+ **dintre, din**) the most inferiority **cel, cea mai puţin** +adj. (+ **dintre, din**) the least

Absolute	**foarte, tare** very	+ adjective
	extraordinar de extraordinary	+ adjective
	prea too	+ adjective

82

Examples:

Radu e **cel mai** bun doctor **dintre** colegii lui.
Radu is the best doctor among his colleagues.

Maria e **cea mai puțin** vorbăreață **dintre** cei patru prieteni.
Maria is the least talkative of the four friends.

Acest bagaj e **foarte greu**.
This baggage is very heavy.

Aceste culori sunt **prea frumoase** ca să fie reale.
These colors are too beautiful to be real.

2. VERBS

The Compound Perfect

The Compound Perfect is formed by combining an auxiliary element (a compacted form of the verb "to have") and the Past Participle of the verb.

1. **am**
2. **ai**
3. **a**
4. **am**   + Past Participle
5. **ați**
6. **au**

Note: The Compound Perfect is used to express a past action and is best translated by the English Past Tense.

Am mers la plimbare.   I went for a walk.

Examples of verbs in the Past Participle form:

a lucra /to work/ **lucrat**; a spăla /to wash/ **spălat**
a vorbi /to talk/ **vorbit**; a dormi /to sleep/ **dormit**
a vedea /to see/ **văzut**; a putea /to be able/ **putut**
a face /to do/ **făcut**; a merge /to go/ **mers**

The Compound Perfect of "to be" and "to have"

TO BE

eu	am fost	noi	am fost
tu	ai fost	voi	ați fost
el, ea	a fost	ei, ele	au fost

TO HAVE

eu	am avut		noi	am avut
tu	ai avut		voi	ați avut
el, ea	a avut		ei, ele	au avut

EXERCISES

1. Describe a visit to a friend.

2. Translate: I had a wonderful evening. We ate too much. The food was very good. This exercise is the most difficult one in lesson 8. The story was too long.

LECȚIA NOUĂ

A FI BOLNAV

Dimineața devreme în camera hotelului.

Mihai: Nu știu ce se întâmplă, dar mă simt foarte rău.

Ana: Te doare ceva? Ești așa palid.

Mihai: Am crampe, sunt amețit și mă doare capul.

Ana: Hai să chemăm recepția să ne trimită un doctor.

A sosit doctorul.

Doctorul: Bună dimineața. Sunt doctorul Ștefan Vasilescu. Ce vă doare?

Ana: Soțul meu se simte foarte rău.

Doctorul: Vă rog să vă sculați și să dezbrăcați bluza de pijama. Dați-mi voie să vă iau temperatura... Da, aveți o ușoară temperatură: 37.6°C*. Tensiunea e normală. Unde vă doare stomacul? Aici? Scoate-ți limba, vă rog. Mulțumesc. Aveți un deranjament stomacal. Ce ați mâncat ieri?

Mihai: Prea mult! Am fost invitați la cină.

Doctorul: Se pare că nu mai sunteți obișnuit cu mâncarea românească. Este delicioasă, dar e foarte grea pentru stomac. Trebuie să țineți regim pentru două zile. Doar ceai, pâine prăjită și cartofi fierți și poimâine vă veți simți mai bine. La revedere.

Mihai: Mulțumesc. La revedere.

---

* The normal body temperature is 36.5-37.0°C. This is approximately 98.6°F.

LESSON NINE

BEING SICK

Early morning in the hotel room.

Mihai: I don't know what's wrong, but I feel awful.

Ana: Do you have pains? You're very pale. Where does it hurt?

Mihai: I have a stomach ache, a headache and I feel dizzy.

Ana: Let's call the front desk and ask for a doctor.

The doctor arrives.

Doctor: Good morning! I'm Doctor Ştefan Vasilescu. What's the problem?

Ana: My husband feels terrible.

Doctor: Please, sit up and take your pajama top off. Let me take your temperature. You have a slight temperature: 37.6° C. Your blood pressure is normal. Where does your stomach hurt? Here? Let me see your tongue, please. Thank you. You have an upset stomach. What did you eat yesterday?

Mihai: Too much. We were invited for dinner.

Doctor: It seems you're not used to Romanian food anymore. It's delicious but very heavy for the stomach. You need a special diet for two days. Only tea, toast and boiled potatoes and the day after tomorrow you should be fine. Good bye.

Mihai: Thank you. Good bye.

VOCABULARY

devreme	early	**crampe**	cramps
ameţit	dizzy	**recepţia**	front desk
vă sculaţi	to get up	**să dezbrăcaţi**	to take off
bluză	blouse	**pijama**	pajama
uşoară	slight	**tensiune**	blood pressure
normală	normal	**obişnuit**	used
ceai	tea	**pâine prăjită**	toast
cartofi	potatoes	**fierţi**	boiled
poimâine	the day after tomorrow		

EXPRESSIONS

mă simt bine (rău)	I (don't) feel well
nu ştiu ce se întâmplă	I don't know what's going on
te doare ceva?	are you all right? (are you sore)
eşti palid	you are pale
mă doare capul	I have a headache
daţi-mi voie	let me...
să iau temperatura	let me take your temperature
aveţi temperatură	you have a slight temperature
scoate-ţi limba	let me see your tongue
se pare	it seems
să ţineţi regim	you need a diet
indigestie	upset stomach
răceală	cold
am răcit	I caught a cold
durere în gât	sore throat
durere de dinţi	toothache
durere de cap	headache

The parts of the body:

cap	head	deget	finger
frunte	forehead	unghie	nail
ochi	eye	piept	breast
nas	nose	plămân	lung
ureche	ear	inimă	heart
păr	hair	stomac	stomach
gât	neck, throat	ficat	liver
umeri	shoulder	picior	foot
mână	hand	coapsă	thigh

GRAMMAR

1. THE POSSESSIVE PRONOUN

Number/ Gender of Object	Singular		Plural	
	Masculine	Feminine	Masculine	Feminine
sing. 1st person	al meu (mine)	a mea (mine)	ai meiale (mine)	mele
plural	al nostru (ours)	a noastră (ours)	ai noștri (ours)	ale noastre (ours)
sing. 2nd person	al tău (yours)	a ta (yours)	ai tăi (yours)	ale tale (yours)
plural	al vostru (yours)	a voastră (yours)	ai voștri (yours)	ale voastre (yours)
sing. 3rd person	al său (his)	a sa (hers)	ai săi (his)	ale sale (hers)
plural	-	-	-	-

Notes:

1. In the spoken language the forms for the 3-rd person are seldom used. Instead the genitive forms of the Personal Pronoun are used.

sing. m.	al lui	a lui	ai lui	ale lui
sing. f.	al ei (his)	a ei (hers)	ai ei (his)	ale ei (hers)
plural m.	al lor	a lor	ai lor	ale lor
plural f.	al lor (theirs)	a lor (theirs)	ai lor (theirs)	ale lor (theirs)

2. The possessive pronoun agrees in number and person with the possessor and in gender and number with the noun designating the object possessed.

Cartea e **a noastră**.	Cărțile sunt **ale noastre**.
The book is ours.	The books are ours.
Băiatul e **al nostru**.	Băieții sunt **ai noștri**.
The boy is ours.	The boys are ours.

3. The possessive adjective is distinguished from the possessive pronoun by the absence of the possessive article.

Cartea **noastră** e aici.	Cărțile **noastre** sunt aici.
Our book is here.	Our books are here.
Băiatul **nostru** e frumos.	Băieții **noștri** sunt frumoși.
Our boy is handsome.	Our boys are hansome.

EXERCISES

1. Pretend to be sick and explain to the doctor what hurts.

2. Translate:

> Our baggage are in the waiting room.
> Yours (2-nd person plural) are heavier than mine.
> My little boy is running faster than theirs.

LECȚIA ZECE

LA UN COCTEIL

Familia Ionescu a organizat un cocteil și a invitat și familia Popescu.

Mihai: Domnule Toma, permiteți-mi să vă prezint prietenii noștri români: Maria și Radu Popescu. Marin Toma, președintele sucursalei române.

dl.Toma: Încântat de cunoștință. Și dumneavoastră vă ocupați cu afacerile?

Radu: Nu. Eu sunt doctor. Lucrați de mult timp cu Mihai?

dl.Toma: Nu, am semnat contractul acum două zile și vom începe să lucrăm de luna viitoare. Până atunci vom termina cu întocmirea și semnarea formelor.

Mihai: Noi construim calculatoarele în Statele Unite și le exportam în România. Sucursala de aici va scrie aplicațiile software pentru piața română.

Radu: Cred că e o idee foarte bună. E momentul potrivit pentru astfel de afaceri. Vă doresc mult succes.

....

Maria: E târziu. Ar trebui să plecăm. Radu, tu trebuie să fii la spital foarte devreme mâine dimineață. Mulțumim că ne-ați invitat, ne-am simțit foarte bine.

Ana: Mulțumim că ați venit. Și noi ne sculăm devreme mâine. Avionul pleacă la ora zece și noi încă nu am împachetat nimic.

Mihai: Ne pare atât de bine că ne-am cunoscut. Poftiți cartea mea de vizită. Data viitoare când veniți în America vă rugăm să ne sunați și pâna atunci să ne scriem.

Radu: Mulțumim. Voi aveți deja adresa și telefonul nostru. Vă dorim o călătorie plăcută. La revedere.

L E S S O N   T E N

AT THE BUSINESS PARTY

The Ionescus have a cocktail party and they invited the Popescus too.

Mihai: Mr. Toma, let me introduce our Romanian friends: Radu and Maria Popescu. Marin Toma , the head of our Romanian division.

Mr.Toma: Nice to meet you. Are you a businessman too?

Radu: No, I'm a doctor. Have you been working with Mihai for a long time?

Mr.Toma: No, we only signed the contract two days ago and we'll start working together next month. By then we should finish the paperwork.

Mihai: We produce computers in USA and we ship them to Romania. Our division here writes the software applications for the Romanian market.

Radu: I'm sure it's an excellent idea. Its the right moment for this kind of business. Good luck.

....

Maria: It is late. We should be leaving. Radu, you have to be at the hospital very early tomorrow morning. Thanks for inviting us. We really enjoyed the party.

Ana: Thank you for coming. We're also getting up early tomorrow. The plane leaves at 10 am and we haven't packed anything yet.

Mihai: It's so nice to have met you. Here is my business card. Next time you come to America please call us and until then let's keep in touch.

Radu: Thank you. You already have our address and telephone number. Have a nice trip. Bye. Good night.

VOCABULARY

a organizat	organized	**președintele**	president
sucursala	division	**lucrați**	you work
vom începe	we will start	**luna**	month
atunci	then	**vom termina**	we will finish
construim	we build	**calculatoare**	computers
va scrie	it will write	**spital**	hospital
am împachetat	we packed	**nimic**	nothing
veniți	you come	**să sunați**	to call
să scrieți	write		

EXPRESSIONS

încântat de cunoștință	glad to meet you
vă ocupați cu afacerile?	are you a businessman too?
am semnat contractul	we signed the contract
acum două zile	two days ago
întocmirea și semnarea formelor	the paperwork
o idee bună	a good idea
aplicație software	software application
piața română	Romanian market
e momentul potrivit	the timing is perfect
vă doresc mult succes	I wish you good luck
e târziu	it is late
poftiți cartea mea de vizită	here is my business card
ne pare bine că ne-am cunoscut	we are glad that we met
data viitoare	next time
vă dorim o călătorie plăcută	we wish you a nice trip

GRAMMAR

1. VERBS

The Future Tense of the Indicative

The Future tense is a compound tense formed of an auxiliary and the Infinitive of the verb.

1. **voi**
2. **vei**
3. **va**
4. **vom**   + Infinitive
5. **veți**
6. **vor**

Notes:

1. The auxiliary is the same for all verbs but varies according to the person and number.

2. When it is part of the Future, the Infinitive is not preceded by "a."

a **mânca** /to eat/   eu voi **mânca**

3. The Future tense can be expressed by using the Present tense with a temporal adverb.

Eu merg mâine în oraș.   I will go to town tomorrow.

The Future of the verbs **to be** and **to have**

to be	**a avea**
eu voi fi	eu voi avea
tu vei fi	tu vei avea
el va fi	el va avea
noi vom fi	noi vom avea
voi veți fi	voi veți avea
ei vor fi	ei vor avea

EXERCISES

1. Describe a business party.

2. Write the future tense for the following verbs:

a călători; a mânca; a scrie; a semna

KEY TO THE EXERCISES

Lesson 1

1. sunt; eşti; e, este; sunteţi; sunt

Lesson 2

2. avioane, ochelari, doctori, fiice, copii, bagaje, paşapoarte, săptămâni, cadouri

3. aveţi, avem, au, ai

Lesson 3

2. al; a; ai; ale; ale

3. unde; cum; când

Lesson 4

2. lor le-am dat; mie îmi place; vouă vă e foame; lui îi trebuie

3. Îmi place camera aceasta. Noi am vizitat unsprezece oraşe. Ei rezervă camera cinci sute optzeci şi doi. Voi puteţi lua autobuzul treizeci şi patru pentru hotel.

Lesson 5

2. Timbrul scrisorii costă o sută şaisprezece lei. Îi dau lui Maria o carte. Poşta e în spatele operei. Bagajul e al soţiei mele. Florile femeilor sunt frumoase.

Lesson 6

2. vă, mă, vă, pentru mine, vă, cu mine, vă, vă, pentru mine, vă, vă, vă, vă, ne, vă

3. Mergi la film? Da merg. Îl iei pe George cu tine? Nu, nu îl iau pe George cu mine, o iau pe Maria cu mine. Noi suntem foarte bucuroşi să-i vedem (pe ei). Ei ne-au invitat la cină.

Lesson 7

2. cumpăr, cumperi, cumpără, cumpărăm, cumpăraţi, cumpără
încerc, încerci, încearcă, încercăm, încercaţi, încearcă

vorbesc, vorbeşti, vorbeşte, vorbim, vorbiţi, vorbesc
vin, vii, vine, venim, veniţi, vin

Lesson 8

2. A fost o seară minunată. (more correct than - Am avut o seară minunată). Am mâncat prea mult. Mâncarea a fost foarte bună. Acest exerciţiu e cel mai dificil din lecţia opt. Povestea a fost prea lungă.

Lesson 9

2. Bagajele noastre sunt în camera de aşteptare. Ale voastre sunt mai grele decât ale mele. Băieţelul meu aleargă mai repede decât al lor.

Lesson 10

2. voi, vei, va, vom, veţi, vor/ mânca, călători /scrie, semna

VOCABULARY

Romanian-English

acasă	home	centru	downtown
acesta	this	a cere	to ask
acela	that	ceva	anything
același	same	cheia	key
acestea	these	chelner	waiter
acolo	there	chiar	even
acum	now	chitanță	receipt
a aduce	to bring	cină	dinner
aeroport	airport	cinci	five
aici	here	cincisprezece	fifteen
a ajunge	to arrive	ciocolata	chocolate
alte	others	a cântări	to weigh
amabil	kind, nice	cât	how (long)
amețit	dizzy	clădire	building
amândoi	both	coafor	hairdresser
an	years	colț	corner
apartament	apartment	a construi	to build
aproape	close, near	controlul	control
a arăta	to show	a conveni	to agree/to
ascensor	elevator		be convenient
a aștepta	to wait	copil	child
a ateriza	to land	crampe	cramps
atâta	so much	a crede	to think
atunci	then	cu	with
a avea	to have	a cumpăra	to buy
a avea grijă	to take care	a cunoaște	to meet/know
avion	airplane	cuplu	couple
		curând	soon
baia	bathroom		
bagaj	luggage	a da	to give
banca	bank	da	yes
băutură	drink	dar	but
a bea	to drink	de	of, from
bine	O.K., good	a declara	to declare
bluza	blouse	delicios	delicious
bucătărie	kitchen	a deschide	to open
bunica	grandmother	devreme	early
		a se dezbrăca	to take off
a cade	to fall	din	from
ca	that	dintru	from
cadou	gift	diverse	different
calculatoare	computers	doamna	Madam, Mrs.
camera	room	doar	only
care	which	doctor	doctor
casa	house	doilea	the second
cartofi	potatoes	a dori	to wish, to like
căci	because	dormitor	bedroom
ce	what	două	two
ceai	tea	a se duce	to go

96

dumneavoastră	you	mare	big
		mașina	car
eu	I	mărime	size
ei	they	meniu	menu
etaj	floor	a merge	to go
excursie	trip	meu	my
		mic	small
familie	family	minunată	wonderful
a fi	to be	a mirosi	to smell
fiert	boiled	mâine	tomorrow
fiica	daughter	mâncare	meal
fiul	son	model	sample
floare	flower	mult	many
foarte	very		
frumos	beautiful	născut,ți	born
		ne	us
a găsi	to find	nevoie	need
greu	difficult	nimic	nothing
graniță	border	noastră	our
ghișeu	counter	normală	normal
		număr	number
haine	clothes	nume	name
hai	let's		
		o	a, an
ieșire	exit	oară	time
imediat	immediately	obișnuit	usual
inclus	included	ochelari	glasses
a invita	to invite	a oferi	to offer
		a opri	to stop
a împacheta	to pack	ora	hour
în	in	orchestra	orchestra
a încerca	to try	a organiza	to organize
a începe	to start		
a închide	to close	pachet	package
a întâlni	to meet	pantof	shoe
întâi	first	a parca	to park
a întârzia	to be late	parcare	parking lot
a se întoarce	to come back	parte	side
înapoi	back	parter	ground level
a întreba	to ask	pașaport	passport
întru	in	a păstra	to keep
a înțelege	to understand	pe	on
		pentru	for
jumătate	half	pereche	pair
		perfect	perfect
la	at	permis	permitted
liniștit	quiet	persoana	person
lângă	near	pijama	pajama
loc	place	pâine prăjită	toast
a lua	to take	poimâine	the day after
a lucra	to work		tomorrow
lucru	thing	plăcut	nice
lună	month	a plăti	to pay
		a pleca	to leave
magazin	shop	podgorie	vineyard

poșta	post office	tensiune	blood pressure
prea	too	a termina	to finish
precis	by all means	timbru	stamp
a pregăti	to prepare	târziu	late
preț	price	tocmai	just
președinte	president	totul	everything
prieteni	friends	trafic	traffic
a primi	to receive	a transporta	to carry
primul	first	a trebui	to have to
a privi	to look	a trece	to pass
profesoara	teacher	trei	three
a putea	to may	a trimite	to send
		troleibuz	trolley bus
raft	shelves		
a rămâne	to stay	țara	land, homeland
recepția	front desk		
a recomanda	to recommend	vacanța	holiday
a recunoaște	to recognize	vamă	customs
renumit	famous	a vedea	to see
repede	hurry	a veni	to come
rest	change	viitor	next
a rezerva	to reserve	vin	wine
rând	row	a vorbi	to speak
româna	Romanian	a vrea	to want
românești	Romanian		
		a se uita	to look
săptămâna	week	un	a, an
scara	stair	unde	where
a schimba	to change	undeva	somewhere
a scrie	to write	unele	some
scrisoare	letters	unu	one
a se scula	to get up	a urma	to follow
sigur	sure	ușa	door
simpatic	nice	ușoara	slight
soneria	door bell		
soț	husband	zborul	flight
soția	wife		
specific	specific		
spital	hospital		
a sta	to sit		
stație	stop, station		
stânga	left		
stop	traffic light		
strada	street		
subsol	underground		
sucursala	division		
sufragerie	living-room		
a suna	to ring, to call		
școala	school		
și	and		
a şti	to know		
tare	loud		

VOCABULARY - EXPRESSIONS

Romanian- English

acum două zile	two days ago
a fost greu?	was it difficult...?
a fost uşor	it was easy...
am semnat contractul	we signed the contract
am rezervat o cameră	I reserved a room
aparat de taxat	taxi meter
aplicaţie software	software application
astă-seară	this evening
a avea nevoie de	to need...
a avea noroc	to be lucky
aveţi ceva de declarat?	do you have anything to declare?
aveţi mărunt?	do you have change?
aveţi nevoie de ceva?	do you need anything else?
aveţi temperatură	you have a slight temperature
bacşiş	tip
bazin de înot	swimming pool
birou cu schimb valutar	currency exchange office
bună dimineaţa	good morning
bună ziua	good afternoon
bună seara	good evening
cabina de proba	fitting room
ce aţi dori...?	what would you like to (order)
ce drăguţ din partea lor	how nice of them
ce mărime?	what size?
a chema un taxi	to call a cab
cât costă?	how much does it cost?
cât face?	how much does it cost?
a completa formulare	to fill out forms
controlul paşapoartelor	passport control
costum de vară	summer suit
cu ce vă pot ajuta?	how may I help you?
cum vă simţiţi în excursie?	how do you like your trip?
culori	colors:

Romanian	English	Romanian	English
alb	white	verde	green
bej	beige	albastru	blue
gri	gray	mov	purple
galben	yellow	violet	violet
roşu	red	maro	brown
portocaliu	orange	negru	black

a se da jos	to get off
data viitoare	next time
daţi-mi voie	let me...
daţi-mi voie să mă prezint	let me introduce myself
daţi-mi voie să vă prezint pe..	let me introduce you to..
de aceea	that's why
de ce nu!	why not!

aş dori	I would like to have
doriţi să comandaţi?	what would you care to order?
dreapta	right
durere în gât	sore throat
durere de dinţi	toothache
durere de cap	headache
e aglomerat	the traffic is heavy
e momentul potrivit	the timing is perfect
e numai bun	it is just fine
eşti palid	you are pale
e târziu	it is late
a face cunoştinta cu...	to meet...
	to make somebody's acquaintance
faceţi dreapta...	take a right
faţaă în faţă	across
formează numărul	he dials
grăbeşte-te	hurry
hai	let's
haideţi!	come on!
hai să mergem	let's go
hai să nu mai fim aşa formali	let's not be so formal anymore
indigestie	upset stomach
îmi pare rău	I am sorry
în cât timp?	how long?
în faţă	in front
în spatele	behind
înainte	ahead
înapoi	back, backwards
încântat de cunoştinţă	glad to meet you
întocmirea şi semnarea formelor	the paperwork
la ce oră?	what time?
lasa-mă să te ajut	let me help you
lateral	sideways, laterally
a lua micul dejun	to have breakfast
o luaţi la stângă...	take a left...
mai vedem noi (informal)	we'll see
magazin cu cadouri	gift shop
mă doare capul	I have a headache
mă simt bine (rău)	I (don't) feel well
a merge la plimbare	to take a walk
a merge pe jos	to walk
mergeţi trei colţuri...	go straight three blocks
mulţumesc (frumos)	thank you (very much)
muzică populară	folk music
ne-a fost greu	it was difficult
ne pare bine că ne-am cunoscut	we are glad we have met

noapte bună	good night
noroc!	cheers!
nota de plată!	the bill (check please!)
nu știu exact	I don't know for sure
nu știu ce se întâmplă	I don't know what's going on
o idee bună	a good idea
o să te sun	I will call you

parts of the body:

cap	head	deget	finger
frunte	forehead	unghie	nail
ochi	eye	piept	breast
nas	nose	plămân	lung
ureche	ear	inima	heart
păr	hair	stomac	stomach
gât	neck, throat	ficat	liver
umeri	shoulder	picior	foot
mâna	hand	coapsa	thigh

pantofi cu tocuri	high heeled shoes
par avion	by airmail
piața română	Romanian market
poftiți	please, here you are
poftiți cartea mea de vizită	here is my business card
poftiți înăuntru	please come in
pot să vă recomand...	may I suggest you...
prea mult	too much
puteți păstra restul	you can keep the change
puteți să-mi spuneți	could you tell me..
răceală	cold
am răcit	I caught a cold
să iau temperatura	let me take your temperature
se pare	it seems
să țineți regim	you need to go on a diet
să strângem masa	let's clear the table
să punem masa	let's set the table
s-ar putea să fie mic	it might be too small
sala de sport	health club
să conducem mașina	to drive the car
scuzați(-mă)	excuse me
se pare	it seems
a servi prânzul, cina	to have lunch, dinner
sunteți foarte amabil	you are very kind
sfârșit de săptămână	weekend
stăpâna casei	the lady of the house
sticlă cu vin	a bottle of wine
stânga	left
te doare ceva	are you all right? (are you sore)
unde vreți să mergeți?	where do you want to go?

vacanță plăcută!	have a nice vacation!
vă doresc mult succes	I wish you good luck
vă dorim o călătorie plăcută	we wish you a nice trip
vă ocupați cu afacerile?	are you a businessman too?
vă place?	do you like?
vă rog	please
vă stăm la dispoziție	let us know
vin dulce	sweet wine
vin sec	dry wine
vreți să încercați?	do you want to try?

VOCABULARY - EXPRESSIONS

English-Romanian

across		față în față	
ahead		înainte	
are you all right?		te doare ceva	
are you a businessman too?		vă ocupați cu afacerile?	
back, backwards		înapoi	
behind		în spatele	
the bill (check please!)		nota de plată!	
a bottle of wine		sticlă cu vin	
by airmail		par avion	
you can keep the change		puteți păstra restul	
cheers!		noroc!	
come in		poftiți înăuntru	
could you tell me..		puteți să-mi spuneți	
cold		răceală	
come on!		haideți!	
colors		culori :	
white	alb	green	verde
beige	bej	blue	albastru
gray	gri	purple	mov
yellow	galben	violet	violet
red	roșu	brown	maro
orange	portocaliu	black	negru

dry wine	vin sec
do you like?	vă plăce?
do you want to try?	vreți să încercați?
do you have anything to declare?	aveți ceva de declarat?
do you have change?	aveți mărunt?
do you need anything else?	aveți nevoie de ceva?
to drive the car	să conducem mașina
excuse me	scuzați(-mă)
fitting room	cabina de probă
folk music	muzică populară
gift shop	magazin cu cadouri
glad to meet you	încântat de cunoștință
good morning	bună dimineața
good afternoon	bună ziua
good evening	bună seara
good night	noapte bună
good idea	o idee bună
go straight three blocks	mergeți trei colțuri...
have a nice vacation!	vacanță plăcută!

to have lunch, dinner	a servi prânzul, cina
he dials	formează numărul
headache	durere de cap
health club	sala de sport
high heeled shoes	pantofi cu tocuri
here is my business card	poftiți cartea mea de vizită
how nice of them	ce drăguț din partea lor
how much does it cost?	cât costă?
how much does it cost?	cât face?
how may I help you?	cu ce vă pot ajuta?
how do you like your trip?	cum vă simțiți în excursie?
how long?	în cât timp?
hurry	grăbește-te
I wish you good luck	vă doresc mult succes
I caught a cold	am răcit
I don't know for sure	nu știu exact
I don't know what's going on	nu știu ce se întâmplă
I will call you	o să te sun
I have a headache	mă doare capul
I (don't) feel well	mă simt bine (rău)
I reserved a room	am rezervată o cameră
I signed the contract	am semnat contractul
I would like to have	aș dori
it is just fine	e numai bun
it is late	e târziu
I am sorry	îmi pare rău
in front	în față
it seems	se pare
it might be too small	s-ar putea să fie mic
the lady of the house	stăpâna casei
left	stânga
let me...	dați-mi voie
let me introduce myself	dați-mi voie să mă prezint
let me introduce you to...	dați-mi voie să vă prezint pe..
let's go	hai să mergem
let's not be so formal anymore	hai să nu mai fim așa formali
let me help you	lasa-mă să te ajut
let me take your temperature	să iau temperatura
let's clear the table	să strângem masa
let's set the table	să punem masa
let us know	vă stăm la dispoziție
may I suggest you...	pot să vă recomand...
money exchange office	birou cu schimb valutar
you need a diet	să țineți regim
next time	data viitoare
passport control	controlul pașapoartelor
please	vă rog
please, here you are	poftiți
parts of the body:	

head	cap	finger	deget
forehead	frunte	nail	unghie
eye	ochi	breast	piept
nose	nas	lung	plămân
ear	ureche	heart	inima
hair	păr	stomach	stomac
neck, throat	gât	liver	ficat
shoulder	umeri	foot	picior
hand	mâna	thigh	coapsa

right	dreapta
Romanian market	piața română
sideways, laterally	lateral
sore throat	durere în gât
summer suit	costum de vară
sweet wine	vin dulce
thank you (very much)	mulțumesc (frumos)
that's why	de aceea
the paperwork	întocmirea și semnarea formelor
the traffic is heavy	e aglomerat
the timing is perfect	e momentul potrivit
this evening	astă-seară
too much	prea mult
toothache	durere de dinți
to need...	a avea nevoie de
to be lucky	a avea noroc
tip	bacșiș
to call a cab	a chema un taxi
to fill out forms	a completa formulare
to get off	a se da jos
to meet/to make somebody's acquaintance	a face cunoștință cu...
to have breakfast	a lua micul dejun
take a left...	o luați la stânga...
take a right	faceți dreapta...
to take a walk	a merge la plimbare
to walk	a merge pe jos
upset stomach	indigestie
we wish you a nice trip	vă dorim o călătorie plăcută
we'll see	mai vedem noi (informal)
weekend	sfârșit de săptămână
what time?	la ce oră?
what would you like to (order)	ce ați dori...?
what size?	ce mărime?
why not!	de ce nu!
what would you care to order?	doriți să comandați?
where do you want to go?	unde vreți să mergeți?
you are pale	ești palid
you have a slight temperature	aveți temperatură
you are very kind	sunteți foarte amabil

Other Romanian Interest Titles from Hippocrene ...

ROMANIAN CONVERSATION GUIDE
200 pages – 5 ½ x 8 ½ – 0-87052-803-3– $9.95pb – (153)

ROMANIAN-ENGLISH/ENGLISH-ROMANIAN STANDARD DICTIONARY
800 pages – 18,000 entries – 4 3/8 x 7 – 0-7818-0444-2 – $17.95pb – (99)

ROMANIAN GRAMMAR
100 pages – 5 ½ x 8 ½ – 0-87052-892-0 – $8.95pb – (232)

TASTE OF ROMANIA
319 pages – 5 ½ x 8 ½ – photos/illustrations – 0-7818-0523-6 – $24.95hc – (637)

ALL ALONG THE DANUBE: RECIPES FROM GERMANY, AUSTRIA, CZECHOSLOVAKIA, YUGOSLAVIA, HUNGARY, ROMANIA, AND BULGARIA
349 pages – 5 ½ x 8 ½ – b/w photos & illustrations – 0-7818-0098-6 – $14.95pb – (491)

... and from Hippocrene's Extensive Slavic Library

AMERICAN PHRASEBOOK FOR POLES, SECOND EDITION
154 pages – 5 ½ x 8 ½ – 12 maps/diagrams/signs – 0-7818-0554-6 – $8.95pb – (644)

AMERICAN PHRASEBOOK FOR RUSSIANS
197 pages – 5 ½ x 8 ½ – 0-7818-0054-4 – $8.95pb – (135)

CZECH HANDY EXTRA DICTIONARY
186 pages – 2,500 entries – 5 x 7 ¾ – 0-7818-0138 – $8.95pb – (63)

CZECH PHRASEBOOK
220 pages – 5 ½ x 8 ½ – 0-87052-967-6 – $9.95pb – (599)

POLISH PHRASEBOOK AND DICTIONARY
252 pages – 5 ½ x 8 ½ – 0-7818-0134-6 – $11.95pb – (192)

RUSSIAN PHRASEBOOK AND DICTIONARY
256 pages – 5 ½ x 8 ½ – 0-7818-0190-7 – $11.95pb – (597)
cassettes (separately): 120 minutes – 0-7818-0192-3 – $12.95 (432)

SLOVAK-ENGLISH/ENGLISH-SLOVAK CONCISE DICTIONARY
360 pages – 7,500 entries – 4 x 6 – 0-87052-115-2 – $11.95pb – (390)

SLOVAK-ENGLISH/ENGLISH-SLOVAK COMPACT DICTIONARY
360 pages – 7,500 entries – 3 ½ x 4 ¾ – 0-7818-0501-5 – $8.95pb – (107)

SLOVAK HANDY EXTRA DICTIONARY
200 pages – 5 x 7 ¾ – 0-7818-0101-X – $12.95pb – (359)

UKRAINIAN PHRASEBOOK AND DICTIONARY
205 pages – 5 ½ x 8 ½ – 0-7818-0188-5 – $11.95pb – (28)
cassettes (separately): 120 minutes – 0-7818-0191-5 – $12.95 – (42)

Prices subject to change without prior notice.

To order Hippocrene Books, contact your local bookstore, call (718) 454-2366, or write to: Hippocrene Books, 171 Madison Ave. New York, NY 10016. Please enclose check or money order adding $5.00 shipping (UPS) for the first book and $.50 for each additional title.